What peopl T0149755

Good Grief

Shelley's wise and compassionate words offer hope and courage, good feelings that are not often associated with grief. Her book written from the perspective of a former nursing career is an empowering, healing dose of essential self-help for all those who are grieving as well as anyone who has ever struggled to face their own mortality. Coping with grief is going to be the theme over the next few years as the world recovers from the pandemic and Shelley is a clear, authentic and uplifting voice that can help people cope better with the trauma.
Theresa Cheung, *Sunday Times* Bestselling Author

Shelley delivers teachings on grief like no other. Her message is warm, compassionate and punctuated with wonderful humour. Whatever is happening in the world, loss and grief are constants. Death ain't going away any time soon, which makes this book a must-read for anyone with a heart. Read, learn, digest, cry, smile and celebrate, all the time being held safely by Shelley's down to Earth approach, supported by her years of experience as a nurse.
Taz Thornton, Author of *Whispers from the Earth*

Shelley is a bundle of sunshine, humour, and professionalism. She was on my podcast, *Going North*, and she lives the message that she writes about. Positive people are still human no matter how long they can smile through adversity. Invite Shelley to speak at your stage whether it's virtual or in-person to share valuable takeaways on being a realistic optimist.
Dominique Brightmon, Bestselling Author and Podcaster

I had such a lovely chat with Shelley on her podcast, and I was immediately delighted by her smile and positive energy. The shifts she is helping make in other people's lives through storytelling and positivity are quite admirable, and I am thrilled to support her in any way possible! I also had a chance to read some of Shelley's work, and her writing is pristine. Clear and concise, with lessons that are truly timeless!

Jordan Gross, Bestselling Author with BenBella Books and Matt Holt Books

Shelley manages to inspire you to live a better life, through her speaking on death. It's an amazing feat – and one she does with an incredible amount of humour – she is properly funny. It was a joy to hear her speak, and I would seek her out to hear her again. Thank you, Shelley!

Kirsten Goodwin, Career Change Specialist

Shelley is a truly inspirational person, she has so much to give. I had the opportunity to listen to Shelley talk about death, the subject no one wants to talk about. Shelley makes this subject so much more comfortable and easier to talk about. She is compassionate, has the right amount of empathy and will hold the audience's attention. I would definitely recommend Shelley without hesitation.

Chad Marshall-Lane, Owner of CML Solutions

I had the pleasure of listening to Shelley speak about death, based on her knowledge through nursing and personal experience with people close to her, and she was captivating and entertaining. Doesn't seem right given the subject matter, but Shelley articulated an intelligent, thought-provoking and unique perspective that got us all hooked.

Her talk was tinged with sadness but masked by humour and humility, and she had us in the palm of her hand. Shelley

is one of the best speakers I have listened to and should you be fortunate enough to hear her speak, you won't be let down, she is a one-off!
Graham Harris, Bestselling Author of *Against the Grain*

A skilled and engaging speaker that manages to tackle the tricky subject of death so beautifully and honestly and yet with a lightness and humour that just has to be seen.

Shelley shares her own experiences both personally and throughout her career as a nurse. Shelley will make you think, laugh and you will leave feeling motivated to live your very best life. Simply fabulous. Highly recommended.
Verity Johnson, Veterinary

The topic of death is one that most people shy away from but Shelley has this ability to speak about the subject in such a great humorous way that puts you at ease whilst tackling the tricky stuff. It was a pleasure to listen to such a natural speaker.
Phillip Mallourides, Global Gold Savers Club and Property

Shelley is an absolute delight with so much energy. I had the most amazing chat and podcast interview with her – and laughter. She is so inspirational and makes you feel amazing too. I love the work that she does.
Zeenat Noorani, Owner of Vida de la Mariposa Coaching

Good Grief

The A to Z Approach of Modern Day Grief Healing

Good Grief

The A to Z Approach of Modern Day Grief Healing

Shelley F. Knight

BOOKS

Winchester, UK
Washington, USA

JOHN HUNT PUBLISHING

First published by O-Books, 2021
O-Books is an imprint of John Hunt Publishing Ltd., 3 East St., Alresford,
Hampshire SO24 9EE, UK
office@jhpbooks.com
www.johnhuntpublishing.com
www.o-books.com

For distributor details and how to order please visit the 'Ordering' section on our website.

Text copyright: Shelley F. Knight 2020

ISBN: 978 1 78904 733 2
978 1 78904 734 9 (ebook)
Library of Congress Control Number: 2020942274

A CIP catalogue record for this book is available from the British Library.

Design: Stuart Davies

UK: Printed and bound by CPI Group (UK) Ltd, Croydon, CR0 4YY
Printed in North America by CPI GPS partners

We operate a distinctive and ethical publishing philosophy in
all areas of our business, from our global network of authors to
production and worldwide distribution.

Contents

Introduction   1

Life   2

Definitions of Life

Life Lessons   3

Life Stages   7

Mini Deaths   10

Definitions of Mini Deaths

A History of Death   12

A History of Dying

Medical Advancements   14

Medical Advancements and Grief   15

Is There Such a Thing as a Good Death?   16

Spiritual Aspects of the Timing of Death   17

Life Between Life   18

Dying   20

Definitions of Palliative Care, End of Life, and Dying

Clinical Observations of the Dying Process

Death   24

Definitions of Death

Causes and Manners of Death

The In-Between States   36

Consciousness

Soul   38

Past Life Regression   40

Life Between Life   42

Future Life Progression

Current Life Regression   43

Coma (Unconsciousness)   44

Near Death Experience   45

Out of Body Experience   46

Shared Death Experience

Grief   **49**

  Grief, Bereavement or Mourning?

  What is Grief?   50

  When Grief Strikes   51

  The Grief Process   52

  Signs and Symptoms of Grief   54

  Grief Recovery Time   57

  Types of Grief   58

  Grief Styles   67

Afterlife   **69**

  Definitions of the Afterlife

  The Soul's Journey   71

  Reincarnation and Past Lives   72

  Life Thereafter   73

  Signs of a Loved One   75

The Grief Voice Box   **78**

  Communication at the end of life and the

  dying stages   79

  Communication after loss and death   86

  The Grief Toolbox   91

  Acceptance   93

  Acupressure   94

  Acupuncture   95

  Affirmations

  Alexander Technique   97

  Angels and Spirit Guides

  Animal Assisted Therapy   101

  Animal Magic   102

  Aquatherapy   103

  Archangels   104

  Aromatherapy Massage   107

  Art Journaling   108

  Art Therapy   110

  Ascended Masters   111

Audiobooks	115
Authentic Movement	116
Ayurvedic Medicine	
Bach Flower Remedies	118
Bibliotherapy	120
Bowen Technique	
Breathwork	121
Bucket List	124
Candles	125
Chakras	128
Change Therapy	136
Cinema Therapy	141
Clairalience	
Clairaudience	142
Claircognizance	143
Clairgustance	144
Clairsentience	
Clairvoyance	145
Cleansing Your Space	146
Cognitive Behaviour Therapy	150
Colour Therapy	151
Community	153
Compassion	154
Complicated Grief Therapy	155
Cord Cutting	
Craniosacral Therapy	157
Crystals	
Dance and Dance Movement Therapy	160
Death Cafes	
Decluttering and Sentimental Upcycling	161
Deities	163
Drama Therapy	165
Dreams	166
Emotional Freedom Technique	168

Energy Bodies and Energy Healing 170
Equine-assisted Therapy 171
Essential and Sacred Oils 172
Exercise 175
Feng Shui 176
Foot Reading 178
Forgiveness 180
Future Life Progression 181
Genealogy 182
Goal Setting 183
Gratitude 184
Guided Vision Therapy 185
Havening Technique
Homeopathy
Hypnotherapy and Self-Hypnosis 186
Indian Head Massage 187
Inner Child Work and Current Life Regression
Iridology 190
Journaling
Journey Work 191
Kinesiology 192
Laughter Yoga Therapy
Life Between Life 193
Life Coaching
Mantras 194
Meaning
Meditation 196
Memory Box 197
Metamorphic Technique 198
Mindfulness
Mother Nature 201
Mudras 202
Music and Sound 204
Naturopathic Medicine 208

Neuro-Linguistic Programming
Nutrition
Oracle Cards   210
Past Life Therapy (Past Life Regression)   211
Permission to Grieve   212
Pilates   213
Play Therapy   214
Podcasts
Poetry   215
Polarity Therapy
Qigong   216
Qoya   217
Resilience   218
Rituals   220
Seitai Therapy   221
Self-Care
Self-Love   222
Self-Healing Touch   225
Shiatsu   226
Smile   227
Storytelling   228
Subconscious Self-Alignment   229
Talking Therapies   231
Thalassotherapy   232
The Emotion Code   233
Thermo-Auricular Therapy
Theta Healing   234
Timeline Therapy   235
Time Management Techniques
Traditional Chinese Medicine   237
Violet Flame   238
Virtual Reality   239
Yoga
Zzzzzzzz for Sleep   240

For Westley, Harrison, Poppy, Milo and Daisy, today and always.

This book is dedicated to all who have shared their life stories and to those of you whose stories are yet to unfold.

Nothing is by chance and it is through beautiful synchronicities that *Good Grief* came to fruition. An eternal heartfelt thank you to Louise and Donna for listening to my story which led to the creation of this book. Absolute love and gratitude to Theresa Cheung for crossing my path with the most angelic timing. And last but by no means least, my husband, Westley, you are all I ever wanted love to be.

Introduction

Death is the only certainty we have in life. It will inevitably come for our friends, family, heart and emotions. Whilst Western medicine will endeavour to fight off death with its medical advancements, ultimately death will still come. Whilst we all busy ourselves with living, on some subconscious level, we know that we are also dying, and yet we rarely choose to think about it, let alone talk about it.

Not many people have a lightbulb moment where they passionately think, "I'm going to write a book about death," but then I am not like most people. In picking up this book, neither are you. We are all individuals with our unique tendencies on how we live, think, and grieve.

Grief tends to be associated very closely with death, but we can grieve over many aspects of our life. This could be a loss of a relationship, job, finances, health, safety, or purpose. All losses – whether it be a way of life or the end of a life – trigger a grief response. All grief is valid and lends itself for a need to step on to an unknown path of recovery.

As a nurse, I worked with patients younger than myself, double my age, some even triple my age, and from all walks of life. Regardless of age or background, we all share the joys, fears, expectations, and hopes about what is important in life. Grief is also common to everyone, regardless of age and experience, and is something that everyone will encounter and look to overcome.

Good Grief: The A to Z Approach of Modern Day Grief Healing does not aim to replace professional help if that is what you need. It is to help provide you with a better understanding of the grief you are facing, and offer clinical and spiritual tools for dealing with grief, as well as suggestions on how to create positive changes as you work through your grief journey.

Life

Definitions of Life

Society speaks so openly about life, but do we truly understand what it is to live? Regardless of your religion, spirituality, or status, nothing in life is permanent, and that includes life itself. Life by dictionary definition is continual change preceding death, but that does not mean that death is the opposite of life, it is part of it. Death is as sacred as birth, and many deaths can be far more gentle than the birthing process. On the wheel of life, some will see both birth and death not as traumatic transitions, but as a spiritual being having a human experience. It is the years between these two major transitions that cause us our greatest pain, as we experience a plethora of life lessons.

To borrow a phrase from Forrest Gump, life is like a box of chocolates; we are all effectively in the same box of life, but we are all different on the inside and out, with each of us becoming a representation of the life lessons within our own unique box. Whilst still running with this strange chocolate analogy, I don't like to take a random dip into a box of chocolates, I like to know exactly what I am heading for, and have often already considered my expectations of what I am looking to experience. Unfortunately, as humans we do not know everything we are going to experience in life, and whilst the unknowns and the voids leave us feeling vulnerable and without a sense of control, how boring and purposeless would our entire existence be if we were foretold the whole story of what was to come, complete with a cast list, a breakdown of the characters, and their roles in our lives?

Depending on your belief system, you may or may not get to choose what life you get. Is it pre-planned, or is it something that is shaped along the way as we make daily choices? Is it never too late to choose our happily ever after? Who truly knows if it is fate, destiny, or just a case of what will be will be? Life can often feel like we have no command over the events around us, but whilst we may believe we have no control, we will always have choices; tea or coffee, stay or go, positive or negative, remaining silent or sharing your story.

When we are making choices we become accountable for our life, and hopefully live a life true to our heart and desires, and not to someone else's thoughts and opinions. When we choose to go for that job, leave that broken relationship, learn that new skill, speak our truth, or travel to that destination, we are creating unique paths through our life, which is the best way to be, regardless of the outcome. Some may fear failure, but I like to think of everything as simply being an experience, not good or bad, just an experience. It is through controlling and making our own choices that we are learning our greatest life lessons, and that is where our greatest potential for growth comes.

Life Lessons

Many years of my healthcare career saw me working with those at the end of life, which to me felt like the most beautiful and privileged role in the world. However, when other people learned what I did for a job, they used to look at me in a way that could only convey a "you poor cow, you must have been really bad in a former life" kind of look. Beyond this pitying look, the words would generally be, "I bet that's a sad job." Yes, at times, it could be. However, we are all humans, and where there is connection, joy and laughter can be found, even in moments of heartbreak, farewells and final breaths.

Through my blessed work as a nurse dealing with the dying, I learned much of life's regrets, what really counts in life, and how to fully live an authentic life. Deep yearnings and big dreams are not exclusive to the young, they are present in the young at heart too. Though many elders had seen more than their fair share of love, loss, and everything in between, many still had dreams they wished to realise.

Many authors before me, and many authors after me, will tell you how they came to learn what the dying regret. There is an absolute poignancy to this, learning how to live by avoiding similar mistakes or choices as made by those who came before us. However, regrets suggest negative connotations, especially when I had so many of my own moments of love and laughter, beautiful stories, practical advice, and plot twists from a life truly lived.

Aside from the focus on regrets, for me, it was apparent that the overall theme felt to be one more of living a life with meaning, which I would categorise into four main types of experiences:

- physical and mental well-being
- belonging and recognition
- treasured activities and memories
- spiritual closeness and connectedness

Holocaust survivor, and psychologist, Viktor E. Frankl wrote his narrative memoir, *Man's Search For Meaning*, about how, in the face of inescapable diversity – such as the threat of losing our life – we come to a great realisation about the importance of finding meaning in our life, and the shift that follows where we turn a personal tragedy into our significant moments of human growth. As Frankl succinctly puts it, "when we are no longer able to change a situation, we are challenged to change ourselves."

But what changes can we make to change ourselves, and in turn move towards our life becoming more meaningful?

Learn from the dying. Heed the words of those who do not have the time to waste life, for they know their time is limited.

It is through spending time with dying patients that I have witnessed the painfully simplistic realisations of what is truly important, and just how integral our emotions are in our everyday life.

Despite our emotions being the foundation of our human condition, we can pass through life unaware of their influence on our cognitive processes: our perceptions, choices, beliefs, motivation, learning, memory and intentions. Having been able to nurse the dying, I have been blessed with the knowledge and wisdom of how to truly live an authentic and emotive life.

Be Happier

Time and time again, those with a suppressed immune system would tell me how they had allowed themselves to be emotionally suppressed throughout their life. The poor want to be rich, the ill want to be healthy, but the rich and healthy simply want to be happy.

Those with a life-changing or life-limiting illness would implore me never to love a broken relationship more than I love myself, to embrace my heart-led dreams rather than a stable pay packet, to be joyous and silly beyond my childhood years, and to find joy in the little things in life. For, when we look back over our life, we will see they were actually the big things all along.

Connect To Something Bigger Than Yourself

It is so easy to be consumed and overwhelmed by self-sabotaging beliefs and thoughts when they are all we have contained within our otherwise brilliant mind. Not everything we think is true, and moreover, our thoughts do not define us.

Whatever you are going through now, take a moment to look beyond yourself. What is it that you can truly believe in? Yourself? God? World peace? Volunteering in your community?

There comes a time in all of our lives when we need to search for meaning and purpose within our life, to help us make our world tangible. Meaning is often derived through connectedness, so begin to make those connections and allow yourself to become part of a greater existence.

Speak Your Truth

Any nurse can tell you that they all have that one patient that they will always remember. For me, it was the poignancy of working with a gentleman who had spent his whole life pleasing others and never speaking out of turn. We connected as I administered his chemotherapy for oesophageal cancer, an iniquitous diagnosis for a man who had never authentically used his voice as he felt he should, and was now being robbed of it for his, now curtailed, future.

I implore you to learn from his choices; speak your truth. Say no to others and yes to yourself. Leap out of your comfort zone with the highest level of self-belief and tell the world your message.

Do More of What You Love

Work less and play more. In the grand scheme of things, you are not going to notice that extra day's pay in your bank balance, but you will feel far richer by saving up happy memories with those you love to be with. The archetypal ward matron would frequently announce, "There are no pockets in shrouds," as she passed by the nursing station and overheard our chatter of our material desires.

We used to think of her as hardened and lifeless, but, looking back, she had already learnt the poignant life lessons from the patients who had shared their dying words with her.

Live Your Life

This may seem a rhetorical term, but you should live your life, not someone else's version or expectations of it.

As I sat administering the colourful flow of cytotoxic agents to those in an inert state, with time, their words and tears would flow with the utmost synchronicity.

The dutiful wife would tell how she had thrown away her dreams to allow others to pursue theirs. The alcoholic who inherited and worked on the family business rather than travel the world. The childless career woman who had given her fertile years to a job she hated but believed it would provide her with the gift of her parents' approval when seen as a success in their eyes.

This is your life – so live it, and move forwards with purpose and meaning each and every day, before there is not enough time left.

I am under no illusion that I am not invincible, any more than I am under the illusion that you will heed the insightful words of the dying I have shared here. However, I ask that you allow yourself the opportunity to at least ponder, in this sacred given moment, just one of those pieces of wisdom; be happier, connect to something bigger than yourself, speak your truth, do more of what you love, live your life.

For now, just pick one and apply it to your day ahead. Just for one day rather than "one day...".

Take that dream and make it bigger, find that person and say, "I am sorry," or simply tell your family that their projections on how to live your life are no longer valid; that you love them but from this day forward you choose to love yourself more.

Life Stages

Our earliest understanding as human beings was the simplicity of a thing called life, which encompassed all of your time before your death. Then came the power of three with childhood, adulthood, and old age. Obviously, with the human love of labelling everything and anything, this came to be extended to even smaller stages and achievements to help mark off the footsteps along our life path: preconception, conception, birth, newborn, toddler, preschool, school age, adolescence, and so on. I am all for celebrating every little achievement in life, and with these numerous stages, I am blessed to have achieved many milestones just from being alive.

Some may resonate with the term stages, others may prefer life cycles, whilst those who are more challenged may view those circles more like a non-relenting spiral of events. Whatever your preferred label, these developmental stages have been created in a world that is ever changing. As greater research and acceptance of a more spiritual existence come about, there are other ways to reflect where you are in life.

In the book, *The Five Stages of the Soul*, Dr Harry R. Moody and David Carroll wrote – through a blend of psychology, myth, religion – reported encounters about what they classed as five stages of the soul, or life as we know it:

- the Call
- the Search
- the Struggle
- the Breakthrough
- the Return

Steve Rother's book *Spiritual Psychology* told us of twelve life lessons, including:

- The Planning Stage (prior to birth)
- First Transition (conception to One Year)
- First Power (two years to early teens)
- Responsibility and Maturity (late teens to late thirties)
- Maturity (forties to seventies)
- Simplification (conclusion of our life in physical form)
- Assimilation (incorporating life experiences into our soul)

Whether you believe in one lifelong journey, five stages, twelve, or an eternal continuum of life, I am a true advocate that we must all endeavour to become the best version of ourselves in all stages of our life, whilst we are privileged enough to be here and able to do so.

Mini Deaths

Definitions of Mini Deaths

The term loss can be rather ambiguous, but it is openly used by healthcare professionals and society alike to describe the death of someone. The deceased did not get lost, they died. Things that are lost have not died, they have been misplaced, overlooked, or temporarily changed. As such, the term loss does not convey the permanency of death. Grief, however, is very much about loss, and loss can come in many forms. When we lose something with which we have an emotional connection to, it is like a mini death. We are left with conflicting emotions following the end or a change to a known way of life, which triggers a grief reaction and the ensuing process.

Mini deaths are grief producing events, and can include: moving home, imprisonment, empty nest syndrome, starting a new school or job, retirement, marriage, divorce, marital reconciliation, end of a relationship (romantic or platonic), end of addictions (alcohol/food/sex/exercise/work), holidays, financial loss or gain, health changes (ourselves and others), pregnancy, sexual issues, change in living conditions, loss of control, loss of identity (job role/change of appearance/parenthood), loss of trust (life-changing event or betrayal), loss of safety (abuse or trauma), loss of approval, or loss of direction or purpose. All of these losses can trigger a grief reaction, and in addition, one loss is rarely one simplistic or isolated loss.

For example, if we look at a loss of health following a cancer diagnosis, the life-changing news is more than just the loss of considering yourself to be healthy and cancer free. Yes, there is the loss of health status, but there may also be loss of certainty, trust, positivity, financial income, sex drive, positive body image, fertility, as well as an influx of emotions, such as denial, anger, bargaining, depression, acceptance, guilt, questioning, confusion, or lack of concentration. There may be weight loss or gain, change of appetite, a time of self-reflection, prioritising what is truly important in your life, and even a change of relationships, as the people in your life will handle your news in different ways. Loss is complex, which in turn triggers complex emotions, just as you would experience or witness in the grief reaction of losing a loved one.

All these stressful life-changing events, along with their associated grief, put our body into a fight-or-flight response. This physiological reaction occurs in response to a perceived harmful event, threat to survival, or attack. When working as intended, this stress response can help you with your focus, alertness, and energy. However, as the nervous system is effectively unable to distinguish the difference between emotional and physical threats, this adrenaline-rich reaction is frequently activated during times of great stress and can make it harder for the fuelled chemical reaction to abate. It is due to this imperfection of the physiological reaction that your response – whether you are experiencing loss of finances or job – can equate to the signs and symptoms of the death of a loved one. Your body is reacting to your emotions and is going all out on protecting you from this variation to your norm.

With every life trauma we encounter, we subconsciously create both an emotional memory and a physical memory, and so whilst emotions may start to bubble up, so might bodily imbalances start to surface. This would manifest as a *dis-ease* in the present, or at a later date in your journey. Whatever form of trauma and upset you have experienced – death or mini death – your grief, along with its plethora of signs and symptoms, are real and will need elements of recovery and healing.

A History of Death

A History of Dying

Just like life itself changes, so do our perceptions of life, dying, death and everything thereafter. Three million years ago, during the Palaeolithic period, our descendants held beautiful metaphysical beliefs about dying and death, believing elements of the individual survived the event of death. Similarly, the Ancient Hebrews believed in the soul, the Ancient Egyptians would mummify to guarantee a fruitful afterlife, and the Ancient Greeks believed in a dual aspect of the soul, whereby one part would continue to live after death. In Ancient times, death was a sacred and spiritual event, but this changed when the Ancient Greeks spoke gravely of their fears of death, which was depicted through mythology, with abundant tales of gods and goddesses being punished for their perceived disobedience in their life. It was only in later centuries, that the Greeks returned to a more spiritual view of death, when Pythagoras wrote how animals share with us the privilege of having a soul, and how every soul was immortal.

During the Middle Ages, death was accepted as a universal destiny shared by all, and whilst feared, it was confronted together as a community. During the Renaissance, despite advancements in terms of societal, financial and political thoughts, death remained very much feared. The seventeenth century took a noted shift from the spiritual understanding to a scientific exploration into dying and death, and these fears continued through into the nineteenth century.

It was during the nineteenth century that we lived in a society where our family simply died at home, surrounded by loved ones. If there were deviations from one's expectations of the dying process, the local doctor or nurse might attend to help calm a crisis or deterioration in condition, but more often than not, we were the experts in our family's transition from life to death. We readily accepted that premature and quick natural deaths were commonplace, and as a family we endeavoured to be present at the last breath.

Medical appointments and interventions were rare, and beyond the family, even the post death routine of funerals were kept as local affairs. It was not unusual for the family to "undertake" the duties of washing, dressing the deceased in their best attire, before a coffin – often made by the local carpenter – would be sourced for a burial.

There were many habits and superstitions that would come into play, windows would be opened to allow the spirit to move on, food and drink aplenty for visitors to the home, widows would be covered from head to toe in black attire, along with the covering of mirrors to prevent the spirit from becoming trapped within the house.

It was through these actions that we assured that the process of dying, and the event of death, was uniquely personal to each family member and their community. It is only over the past one hundred years that death has become ignored, feared, and depersonalised. Death is now seen as an encroachment of life, rather than a part of it.

Dying and death began to move from our familiar place of our own homes and into care homes, retirement and assisted-living communities, hospitals, and hospices, which in turn separated us from the reality of dying and death. When dying is managed by healthcare professionals rather than family members, we become more fearful of dying, death, and how to act should we be with the dying.

We have all become so busy "living" be it through working, sleeping, exercising, eating, or raising families, that we lose touch with death. Seeing death falling under the remit of a clinical setting, where care is available twenty-four hours a day, family and friends have become shielded and detached from the reality of what happens to the dying. It could be argued that this shift creates protective measures of our emotions in the grieving process, as we can detach from the sights, sounds, smells and other areas of death. But with this, we also deny ourselves an insight that cannot be truly learned any other way.

Medical Advancements

Societal changes have caused a shift whereby there have been reductions in deaths from infectious disease due to universal vaccinations, but an increase in death due to suicide, violence, and accidents. Despite ongoing medical research and early diagnosing, cancer remains accountable for twice as many deaths in recent years than it was when the National Health Service (NHS) was founded back in 1948. It is as if the medical interventions are preventing and delaying many pathological processes, but society, and its new ways in life, lends itself to a plethora of ways in which to die.

It is often argued that when we are prolonging life through medical interventions, we are simply living longer but with more comorbidities. It was only recently, in 2015, that irreversible brain disorders such as Alzheimer's disease and vascular dementia were cited as causes of death for the first time ever. This may be due to having been previously classified as a natural part of the aging process, or because dementia was now being attributed to other illnesses that an individual presented with.

There have been so many positive medical advances, from pharmaceutical discoveries, surgical innovations, precision medicine, regenerative therapies, and technological advancements. These advances in medicine have truly transformed the trajectories of our lives, and in the main, for the better of mankind. However, as with most aspects of life, there is the counterbalance argument proffering that our modern way of dying is like a managed dying process, with so many clinical interventions now pushing death's door further down our life path, which raises the question of whether such progress is providing quantity over quality.

Maybe it is modern medicine's attempt to soften death by prolonging life through its interventions. Who is to say what is right or wrong with these medical advancements? Some will be grateful for the extended time with their loved ones, others may grow fearful over a sense of loss of control in their own life as they become dependent on medicine. Whether it is a positive or negative, it is without argument that modern medicine has played a vital role in how we now die, and how the dying process affects loved ones, friends, and family. This in turn affects the way in which we go on to grieve.

Medical Advancements and Grief

When I studied my nursing degree back in 2001, the teachings of grief were brief, and accounted for about three presentations: normal grief, absent grief, or delayed grief. Grief was categorizable. Here we are just two decades later, and partly as a result of many medical advancements and interventions, our understanding of grief is far more complex. There are now believed to be around eighteen different types of grief.

One of these new forms of grief is anticipatory grief, where an impending loss, such as a long-term illness, initiates the grief process in the anticipation of the final event of death. On a positive note, families may be able to find closure, reconcile differences, and have the chance to say goodbye, now that death is more controlled. However, what is often seen is heightened emotions, such as anger, as we may feel we are being given a sense of false hope and the denial of a natural death. I am not here to debate what is right or wrong, simply to highlight the ripple effect of dying and death due to medical advancements in more recent times.

Is There Such a Thing as a Good Death?

Death may come in a swift and unexpected manner, a deterioration into frailty or from a life-limiting illness, or even come as a wish if your choice is euthanasia. So, with these ways and many more in which we can die, is there a way of defining what is considered to be a good death?

We can all agree that sudden or violent ends to life are not what we would want for our loved ones. However, if we are ready or accepting of our death, and have made our own informed choices, then what is perceived as a good death could be achievable. Whilst it is important to endeavour to lead a good life, it could be said that it is more important that we aim for a good death, as we only have one moment to get it right.

Within palliative care, it is said that a good death can be achieved in the context of the individual's clinical diagnosis and presentation of symptoms, with the addition of specific social, cultural and spiritual wishes being met, whilst taking into consideration patient and family wishes along with professional expertise.

But what is a good death from the perspective of the dying?

One of the key elements to a good clinical death is maintaining control of matters we can manage. My hospital patients would express their dying wishes as effective and tailored pain management, informed choices of treatment, maintaining dignity, quality of life not quantity, psychological support, a sense of completion in life, religious and spiritual needs being met, and their family being present.

Sadly, we cannot always guarantee a good death, as often life ends without warning, or before our heart feels ready to let go of a loved one. I have seen so many people struggle with life after loss, not just from the void in their life, but the emotions and questions that fill their hearts, minds, and days as a result of being unable to achieve a good death. I am not going to harshly declare that things happen for a reason, but I would like to offer you comfort from a spiritual aspect of the timing of death.

Spiritual Aspects of the Timing of Death

Our human spirit is stronger than we may ever realise in this lifetime, but as a former nurse, I have seen its potential when working with those facing life-changing diagnoses and at the end of their life. Those who may have previously been perceived as meek and mild can conjure up the greatest strength to defy the odds, beat an illness, or hold on to their last breath whilst their loved ones travel from the other side of the world to be with them.

This determination of spirit to hold on to life can also be utilised to finish their life in unexpected moments. For example, when the watchful family members finally step away for a refreshment, so that the loved one has a moment of unwitnessed actions and finally undertakes their final gasp of earthly air. Your loved ones do not suddenly leave to make you feel guilty or leave you with unanswered questions for the rest of your days; they leave because they do not want you to witness the finality of their lifetime and to commit it to your memories, and because they do not wish for loved ones to experience anxiety or despair due to the end being imminent. Please know and trust me when I say that your loved one left when it was right for you both, they were ready to accept the end of their illness and life, and in a final act of protection, took their final breath without your bated breath. Remember them when they were living and breathing, not when they were too tired to create new happy memories. The dying choose to go when they feel it is the most beautiful and peaceful time to go. For those who may not have reached a place of acceptance in terms of their earthly incarnation drawing to a close, they are greeted by an energy or loved one to help them transit. We are never alone at the point of death, even if we appear to be in an empty room.

Many ancient scriptures suggest that our days are of a fixed number and cannot be exceeded, but then it could be said that there is a profound difference between God's omniscience and our own free will. Sometimes we can draw comfort through the timing of death, be it at the time or later in our life. My beautiful stepdad died suddenly on 1st January without warnings or a final goodbye. However, he always liked things to be just so, and ended his earthly existence on the first day of the first month having started his earthly incarnation on an equally balanced 4th day of the 4th month which made my mum smile at the synchronicity despite her internal pain.

I know that if you are in the midst of your grieving journey right now, little comfort or wisdom can be bestowed upon you to reassure you that the timing was right, as the heart will never feel ready for such a loss as you are experiencing right now. I am just sharing my observations that many aspects of our life, and subsequent death, may be predetermined. This may be around the numerology of the death date, when you are not fully engaging and evolving in life like you agreed to in your life between life, or the completion of your preselected life lessons.

Life Between Life

Through my work as a past life regressionist, I believe that before your soul comes into existence in this incarnation, there is the life between life process where we agree and sign up for what life lessons our soul should learn, and what karmic debt requires payment in order to evolve further in our next earthly incarnation. The Universe will keep giving you the same old lessons over and over again until you finally overcome and master the teachings needed for your highest good. To exemplify, these lessons can see us changing from a perpetrator in a past life to the victim in this life, or perhaps able-bodied in the past but less able in this life, from rags to riches, or jilted in the last life but more empowered in this incarnation so not codependent on another. It is proffered, and I have witnessed, that we get to select many choices before we agree to incarnate again, and this includes our parents, creed, colour, body shape, location, and lessons. Once we are birthed into this life, we experience a sense of amnesia, where all our previous life knowledge and wisdom is still within us, but is only slowly revealed to us as we learn and evolve as an individual in this life.

As I stepped away from my clinical roles into my spiritual practices, I used to wonder how the medical advancements that moved the goalposts around dying would manipulate one's predetermined life path. However, having observed and learned what I now know, there is a great truth in the words "everything happens for a reason". From a spiritual aspect of predetermined lessons, sometimes the shortened and prolonged earthly experiences are all part of the life lessons across multiple lives.

I know some of you will be reading these words in the midst of your own pain, and thinking death has nothing to do with numerology, spirituality, belief, rhyme or reason, it simply just is. Death is an ever-present possibility for each and every one of us; whether we are four or one hundred and four, death is always possible. And you are absolutely right, so let us bring this book back to you and your grief journey, as we step into our next chapter together.

Dying

Dying is the process which leads to the final event of death but it is often a concept or time of great ambiguity or confusion, so let us now look at key terms and some clinical and spiritual symptoms around dying.

Definitions of Palliative Care, End of Life, and Dying

As with many terms in related fields, some of the keywords are used interchangeably, but I wish to provide you with clarification of the difference of palliative care, end of life, and dying, so that it may help simplify matters for you during what can be an overwhelming time.

Palliative care encompasses the control of physical, emotional, social and spiritual care, and this type of care is accessible and provided at any stage when a person has received a diagnosis of a life-limiting condition.

End of Life (often seen as EoL) provides all of the patients with the same aspects of palliative care, but relates to the last stage of life, so is now known as a limited prognosis, as opposed to a life-limiting condition.

Dying is the active process preceding the event of death, which is now expected to occur within the following weeks, days, or hours.

Clinical Observations of the Dying Process

All heart-led frontline healthcare workers will be exposed to complex emotions within their job role, due to the nature of working with people during their most vulnerable and emotional life experience. Within the remit of end-of-life care, being a healthcare professional leads itself to a complex and multifaceted role with heightened emotional exposure. However, professionals have an invisible boundary of empathy, which prevents falling head and heart into the dying process of someone else's loved one.

I once worked with the most knowledgeable and yet most humorous palliative care nurse, who had become so accustomed to recognising signs of the dying, she found herself in work mode even when she was on holiday, analysing people around the poolside, placing her bets on who would be dead by the end of the year. Book in one hand, drink in another, whilst scanning the poolside asking, "Would I be surprised if this person died within the year?" She told me about the scientific and medical research on illness trajectories that could be applied to most patients. Factors such as four or more hospital admissions in one year, serious episodes of health deterioration, and prolonged dwindling of certain signs and symptoms, and we shall look at these now.

Whilst everyone's deterioration will be different, there are displayed symptoms that are widely recognised as part of the dying process. I have witnessed time and time again, particularly in elderly medicine and oncology nursing, how patients start to find simple activities of daily living exhausting months prior to their death. Tasks, such as getting up from an armchair and walking to climb into bed, can become an overwhelming and exhausting exercise. Even the art of conversation can start to show signs of tiring. A dying person may start to withdraw from watching or reading the news, avoid trivial small talk, disengage from their usual activities, and instead rest or sleep more.

Whether the subtle shifts are physical, emotional, or social, the decline in energy levels is the knock-on effect of deteriorating brain function and our metabolic processes. As with all aspects of human life, each and every one of us is different, so there will always be variations from the norm. For example, when treatment is withdrawn at the end of life, the body will initially draw from its own reserves, but each patient and disease process will act differently. Some will die within minutes, others in hours, days, or even weeks.

As the deterioration continues while the patient moves from months to days before their death, the signs and symptoms become more apparent. Due to the further deterioration of brain function, other bodily processes alter. Blood circulation slows, urinary and faecal output change, delayed swallowing reflexes and coughing, varying body temperature, electrolytes and chemicals start to imbalance, all of which can create disorientation, confusion, hallucinations, or agitation. Despite all my years in nursing, even up to my last nursing shift, I found it difficult to truly differentiate which behaviour some patients were displaying. With the voice of the patient weakened or lost, they would be unable to communicate their emotional state, which is why comfort is key at the end of life, both in terms of the physical and the emotional.

As the final days turn to the final hours, there are more changes that can be observed in the process of dying. The most common symptoms, and often the most alarming and upsetting for the onlooker, is when the breathing patterns and volume changes. The charmingly known "death rattle" is simply a collection of secretions that have pooled at the back of the throat, but due to a slowing swallow reflex, is not being moved as it would have naturally been done just hours or days beforehand. Playing gentle music to help blend in with the noise can help, if you feel unable to fill the air with conversation around your loved one, as I know many family members have their own lump in their throat and an inability to swallow as the imminent death lingers around them.

With equally upsetting presentation, as well as the gurgling sound of their breaths, there is a change to the patient's regular breathing pattern as the respiratory processes begin to slow. Cheyne-Stokes breathing is when the patient takes a breath, or even several breaths, and then there is a pause. This pause may seem like eternity for the family members gathered around, but then the patient will take another breath. However, this pause is a true sign that their last breath will soon be here.

As the circulatory system begins to slow even further, the heartbeat and peripheral pulses become more faint and harder to find. Their skin may start to appear clammy, and to look mottled, or have a cyanosed blue tinge to it, beginning at the extremities, as the body starts to slowly close down from the furthest reach inwards.

It is said that the eyes are the window to the soul, and when nursing the dying, I wholeheartedly believe this. I have sensed that the soul has long passed by the time many patients have reached this stage of death where the body begins to slow down. The eyes often appear glazed-over; a solitary tear may form, but I had often noticed an absence behind the eyes as if the soul of the body has silently and secretly left, leaving only its body shell behind for the bereaved to connect with, and for formalities of a human death to follow.

Whilst it may be hard to hear that we are more than our physical body whilst in the midst of your own grief, I believe that there is more to us than our human existence alone.

In Chapter Six, The In-Between States, we will be looking more deeply into the spiritual dying process in terms of state of consciousness. If this alternative view is not for your heart and mind, you can move on to Chapter Seven on Grief, as I know and appreciate that is why this book is resting in your hands and that grief is present in your heavy heart.

Death

By this point we have encountered the word death many times, both in the text, and in our own personal life. But in a nutshell, what is death?

Definitions of Death

A physical death is the irreversible cessation of all our vital biological processes, as indicated in the permanent stoppage of our cardiac, circulatory, respiratory and brain functions. The heart, the blood flow, the breathing, and the brain all stop, as does life on earth. The determination of death is measured by accepted medical standards, which include listening for heart sounds, feeling for a pulse, assessing for signs of breathing, any response to pain or verbal instructions, and checking the eye responses.

Dying is considered to be a physiological process, with death being classed as the final event in the process. When death takes away someone that was important in life (whether they were loved or not), everything physical is removed and only a memory can remain in its place. These memories can be strong and controlling, and may even distort the truth at times, softening both the past and the present reality. No one likes to talk about death but it will eventually come to us all, through one of its many forms and guises. Whilst it may be difficult, let us take the time to look at the different ways in which death can occur.

Causes and Manners of Death

A cause of death is the one specific injury or disease that led to the event of death, and the manner of death is how the specific injury or disease led to the death, which can be classified into five categories: natural, accident, suicide, homicide, and undetermined.

Suicide

I am a passionate, non-conformist who is driven to create a world where we speak as openly about life as we do death. With this is mind, it comes as no surprise that I am starting with what remains one of the most taboo subjects in the arena of death – suicide. Suicide is one of the most heartbreaking tragedies that the human spirit can endure, and the need for society to try and be more open and supportive around this subject is paramount.

Statistics tell us that someone dies to suicide every forty seconds. That's three thousand per day. And yet society tends to forget or ignore that such things happen, and the subject itself carries a social stigma. If you thought people avoided mouthing the word "death", the word suicide takes that feeling to a whole new level.

Any death pulls us out of our everyday mundane existence and into a temporary place of endless questions, to which there are often no clear answers. All deaths leave us with this aftermath of emotions, but when a friend or family member commits suicide, those left behind are plunged into additional entangled emotions of confusion, guilt, and over-analysis. When someone close to you ends their life this way, your entire trusted life, thoughts, and belief systems become subject to scrutiny. The grief for the suicide survivors can be more complex and traumatic than what is considered to be normal grief, and can led to anger, guilt, shame, and even post-traumatic stress disorders.

As a student nurse I remember working nights which can be unsettling enough in itself, what with the low lighting, a sense of stillness, and an eerie silence. I will always recall how I returned from my break to see the shocked faces of my mentors that were hiding an untold truth. Had I made a drug error? Has someone broken my favourite mug? No, a patient had tried to commit suicide behind their drawn curtains, and the qualified staff members seemed awash with maternal emotions and seemed to want to protect me from this unforeseen event. There I was, embarking on a career which would inevitably involve loss of health and life, and still people felt I should be protected from this attempt at self-inflicted death.

Attempted suicides continued to pepper my career path, as I went on to nurse patients who had attempted suicide but survived. I have nursed those who have tried to end their life through a drug overdose, hanging, jumping off buildings, stabbing, electrocution, poisoning, shooting, and crashing their car. When you survived a suicide attempt, two paths seemed to open; some would view their survival as a rebirth of this incarnation, whilst others would find the irreversible damage to their body only added to their initial emotional pain and made life even more unbearable.

From what I have seen, and from what has been shared with me, suicide is rarely a singular issue but moreover an accumulation of problems or losses, such as financial changes, relationship problems, or a variety of similar issues. Put simply, suicide can occur when one feels life is too much or not enough. There is a very thin line between those who commit suicide and those who do not. I have come to realise that suicide is not so much a line between each of us as individuals, but rather a thin line within each and every one of us.

Murder

When death occurs due to murder, the grief may be more difficult to deal with than loss due to the aging process or disease. Similarly to suicide, there are always so many unanswered questions of "why", which will only ever remain truly known by a third party. All grief is emotional, but with murder there seems to be elevated levels of anger and shock, and in the midst of all this is the fact that it is a crime. The loss of an individual through murder – due to the shock of the situation – can create a ripple effect, whereby the emotions expand beyond the immediate family, and out into the local community and beyond – perhaps even nationally and globally – which may lead to grieving in the public eye. Your grief is no longer your grief, it becomes a shared grief within communities and society at large.

Sudden Death

Sudden death can happen in the blink of an eye. In a bad analogy, it is like the tablecloth trick where a tablecloth is whipped out from underneath a normal-looking table full of objects. The tablecloth is no longer there, but everything else is left behind, looking relatively untouched by what has just happened. Did it really happen as everything else still appears the same? What did I miss? When was the last time I truly looked at this? Was there anything I should have known?

I have noticed the emotions of the remaining family displayed in cases of sudden loss, and how they have parallels to those who have experienced a loss through suicide. There is a lot of analysis of what could possibly have been missed, what could have been done differently, and a desperation to recall the last conversation. I have also observed how, when people have been lost to sudden death, there is a new inherited belief that you can no longer trust anything in life; that nothing is safe. One of the greatest pains is that death will end a life, but not the relationship, that will remain in the heart and minds of those still here on earth. Sudden death is not exclusive to individuals either, as there are cases of road traffic accidents or mindless violent attacks, where many family members can die at once, resulting in horrific multiplied effects of shock and loss.

Even mini deaths in our life can be sudden mini deaths, where no one actually died, but a sense of security and known way of life is suddenly stripped away. Domestic violence, anaphylactic reaction, a diagnosis, emergency surgery (amputations, hysterectomy, colostomy, tracheostomy): these forms of death and loss can also trigger a grief reaction within our life. A life that we may not have foreseen or wished for ourselves.

Aging Associated Disorders

Old age is not a diagnosis or what you would see documented on the death certificate for the cause. You would expect the doctor to write the cause of death was cardiac arrest or respiratory failure, as the heart beats for the last time, or the body takes its last breath. The body has finally come to a halt after years of blood pressure variations, heart beats, joint usage, trauma, or hard work.

My grandparents' generation used to say "they had a good innings" as an expression of an acceptable death given that the friend had survived for many decades. Nowadays, as we discovered in the A History of Death chapter, we live in a time where – due to medical advancements and interventions – we are living longer than ever before. It is with this shift in medical interventions, that we are sometimes gifted with additional time with loved ones, compared to generations before us. However, death will come for us all, and grief will naturally follow as we lose the one we love, regardless of the age.

Long-term Illness and Palliative Care

Similarly to a life prolonged, when we receive a diagnosis of a long-term illness, we have a sense of time to say goodbyes, but this is not to say that the grief we experience is diluted. When we or our loved ones are diagnosed with conditions such as cancer, multiple sclerosis, heart failure, or Alzheimer's disease, to name but a few, death becomes the elephant in the room. We strive to find a workable balance between normal daily life and the knowledge that death is tiptoeing towards our loved one. As with many observations through my nursing career, news of a palliative or long-term condition can be handled two ways; some will see life as a timebomb and become overwhelmed, others will embrace the precious remaining lifespan for discovering just how beautiful life can be from the vantage point of death.

Healthcare professionals are often confronted by emotional family members, insisting that they do not tell their loved ones of their diagnosis. Dear reader, please know that even without a clear diagnosis, no one knows themselves better than themselves, so your loved ones will already know or sense that they are unwell or dis-eased, and this withholding of truth can be damaging to many individuals as well as preventing a good death. Those with a time limit may still have dreams they wish to pursue, words they wish to be heard, and practicalities they wish to sort for peace of mind. As such, it is imperative they are given the chance to do so whilst they are still able to do so. Whilst health trajectories are not one hundred per cent in their accuracy, they can often provide a timeframe of that which we have left. In palliative care and life-limiting illness, there is often the chance to help loved ones fulfil their wishes, a privilege denied to those who experience a sudden ending to their life.

Whilst it is important to have discussed my clinical observations, we are more than our medical team and trajectories, so our spirit, mindset and wishes should never be disregarded or undermined. Our human existence is powerful, but our spirit – our intellect, emotions, fears and passions – are even stronger, and this is why I mentioned the importance of being truthful with our loved ones around their diagnosis and prognoses. Our human spirit is a powerful tool within each of us; so, whether we choose to give up or carry on, it will inevitably guide us to our desired outcome. Life is full of choices, but so is death.

Miscarriages, Stillborn, and Newborn death

As we discussed earlier, we readily accept that the old naturally outlive the young, but when a life hasn't even come to an external life, grief can be insurmountable. When a pregnancy or baby dies, so do their parents' wishes, hopes, and dreams. No one can know if it is more painful to lose a known person and personality, or one where their greatness and story is left unfolded and untold.

Miscarriages, stillborn, and newborn deaths cause a pain that is unheard of and unfamiliar to most, and understood by few, although in reality, experienced by so many. Parents feel a strong unconditional love for their conceived yet unborn child, a secret and unbreakable bond. To lose their precious creation to the destruction of death before they ever had a chance of a life experience can seem numbing, unjustified, and beyond cruel. Parents are left with an empty womb, empty heart, and empty arms. The innocence and safety of pregnancy is stripped from you, and you may never trust a conception, pregnancy, outcome, or life itself again.

Miscarriages are a silent pain, at the time, and every day thereafter for the foreseeable future. You have created a life to become a parent, and then you are stripped of this anticipated life. Are you still a parent? What if this was your only chance at parenthood? If you are not worthy of the label "parent" then does this belittle their brief existence? And, in the midst of all this, parents need to allow themselves to grieve for what never came to fruition, often a hidden grief, as not many would have learned of the expected life to come.

Abortion

When I produce my articles, books and podcasts, I come from a place of love, where I endeavour to help as many people as possible to move on in their sacred life, particularly following a life-changing event. Whilst I know people will find the topic of abortion a difficult read based on their own experiences, religion, beliefs, morals and ethics, I feel driven to mentioning this as a form of death.

The women who have experienced abortion told me how

they still underwent grief and its entangled emotions as with any loss of life, but it was a lonelier path they trod, as they were alone due to perceptions of others for them being a murderer, a failure, or simply physically alone due to the breakdown of a relationship.

Whilst the body of the person may appear to heal after an abortion, the psychological scarring can remain like an open wound. Many women express anger and self-loathing for having aborted a child, sometimes because it was not their choice but an ultimatum from another, be it a partner or medical practitioner, with the negative emotions consolidating even further, should they experience fertility issues in the future.

Euthanasia

Euthanasia, or assisted suicide, may be considered to be on a par with the taboo subject of abortion, with many arguing if you can legalise abortion at the start of a life, choices should be extended as an option at the end of the life cycle. Others will be against euthanasia, saying that it is not a natural death, but then others would proffer that due to surgery, medication, and other medical interventions, death is no longer a natural event, and just like euthanasia, is a form of medical-assisted dying.

Relationships and Death

Children

There is something within society that makes the death of an elderly parent the easiest-to-digest death. In the natural order of the aging process, it is a given that the older generation will die before the younger; the parents will die before the children. Maybe this is why when the universal laws are reversed, and parents outlive their children, the pain can feel unconquerable. All those unknown achievements, milestones, dreams and now impossible years are lost in an unknown void of what could have, and should have been. This is indeed one of the areas where I have seen the bargaining stage of Elisabeth Kübler-Ross's grief model, when either following a life-changing diagnosis or upon death itself, parents will fervently bargain and barter anything, to replace the child's prognosis or lost life.

In the midst of the anguish, so many questions form in a bid to make sense of it all. What if your child was your only child, the one person that turned you from a couple to a family? Who are you now? How are you known? Are you still a parent? All of these questions only serve to consolidate the pain, regardless of the years that may have passed.

Parents

The bond between a parent and child is one of the most fundamental human connections we have. Is it worse to lose a parent you never came to know, or to lose a parent who you knew and loved? I would argue neither, as all losses related to our key role models are tragic and rob us of a relationship we are most worthy of. Whether you had a brilliant, awful, or indifferent relationship with your parents, your emotional connection with them was probably a strong bond, due to the wonder of unconditional love. When a parent dies, part of our identity can die too, as part of our genetic make-up is severed, leaving us alone with our thoughts and memories of who we are.

Children can undergo different grief patterns, often depending on their own age at which the parent died. How others treat the child, regardless of their age, can vary from an upbringing of pity and being treated as special, through to being bullied for being a variant from the norm. In later years, some children are drawn to partners who fulfil qualities their life lacked from an absent parent, whilst others search for a greater understanding of self by learning their parents' traits from people who were privileged to have known them.

In the grief of the person whose parent is deceased, whether they are a blood relative, carer, or someone who fulfilled a parental role, there are other facets that may impact on your own grief, such as the grief process of the surviving parent, siblings, aunties, uncles, and other connections. Your mere presence can be a trigger for others' own grief, when they see the deceased one's resemblances in your face, mannerism, and general being. For some families, the loss will create family conflicts, whilst others will be drawn closer together.

Siblings

It is proffered that during the earlier stages of our life, the sibling bond is stronger than that which we share with our parents, so consequently, the sibling bond is believed to be one of the most important relationships in our life; shared genes, upbringings, and secrets. In fact, the only force powerful enough to cut short the friendship between siblings is death.

When both our parents die we become an orphan. If our husband or wife dies we become a widow. But what is it you become when your sibling dies, are you still a brother or a sister? Of course you are, but this void and speaking in a past tense can bring about a plethora of thoughts and emotions, and can trigger thoughts about our own mortality.

Loved and Unloved Ones

Children, parents and siblings are all examples of death that results in a loss in our life, but with this subtitle of loved ones, I refer to losing one with whom we had a romantic relationship. This can be a current or past relationship, a new relationship spanning a few weeks or a long-term one spanning years or decades, a happy relationship or troubled connection. On some level, at some point in time, an emotional connection external to our bloodline was formed and there were shared moments of love.

When a loved one dies we often lose more than one label of partner, they could be our best friend, our rock, and our support network. Many will refer to their partner as their "other half" which, when death appears, can lead to us feeling like we are lacking in wholeness, and we may struggle with our true identity, as we have come to live as half of a double act, losing sight of who we are as a unique individual.

Each and every grief will be different depending on the distinct relationship you shared, some will be swept away in a tidal wave of emotions, whilst others may draw relief from the new path ahead. All I can do is to reassure you that just like the moon, no matter what phase you find yourself in, you are still whole.

Friends

Aristotle described a deep friendship as "one soul in two bodies". The death of a friend can be a complex matter, and one of which we may have to face many times. The bond we share with our friends can be as strong as relationships we share with our own family members. It is often our friends who we turn to during challenging times, and can help us to gauge a better understanding of ourselves.

When a friend dies, one of the difficulties is the one person you would naturally talk to is the very person that has died. The death of a friend has many factors, and can include feeling isolated by the death, rejected by the friend's family, concerns over forming new friendships, negative thoughts due to crossed words or missed opportunities, or even considering your own mortality.

Work Colleagues

There are taboos within the workplace, and death and grief is one of them, so what happens when a work colleague dies? Grief can come with an air of openness, given the mutual connection of the lost colleague. Unlike when we experience a personal loss and our co-workers struggle with the right words to voice, when you are all sharing the same loss, a collective grieving process can commence.

The death of a work colleague should not be underestimated, given how much time we share within our working week, where together we can laugh, complain, celebrate our life with them. For many of us, depending on our support network, we may consider our co-workers to be our closest friends, sometimes even view them as the family. Regardless of whether you were close friends or just a daily acquaintance, you may be affected and need to work through your grief in the very environment you would normally connect with them.

The In-Between States

It is all a matter of consciousness; our waking life, sleeping, dreaming, meditating, alive or deceased. Discussions around human consciousness after life are becoming more commonplace in both wider society and in scientific research which presents theories of what happens to our consciousness beyond our physical death. However, in this chapter, we are going to be looking into our consciousness activity whilst we are living, and the various ways in which we can discover that we are more than just our human existence. There is extensive scientific research around profound spiritual experiences which can occur within the veil between life and death, as well as between the states of being awake and asleep, so let us discover more about consciousness and these spiritual experiences.

Consciousness

Consciousness in its simplest definition is the self-awareness of all of your internal and external existence: any experience, feeling, cognition, or perception you have. Without consciousness, nothing is experienced, neither inside of us nor beyond our physical body. This description is vast in scope, and covers everything from the last song you heard being stuck in your head, to the unconditional love felt in a hug, or the blessed insight from a meditation. Consciousness is something which we all share; each one of us has awareness, it is only our perspectives and conditioning that make us believe we are so different to one another.

Consciousness may sound like an idiosyncratic label used exclusively by mystics, witches, saints, or sages, but an awareness of consciousness has been around for as long as Homo sapiens themselves. Despite its ancient roots, consciousness carries an air of ambiguity in terms of a succinct definition, and an uncertainty around how many different states of consciousness there are. Nonetheless, for the purpose of this guidebook, we shall name seven.

Waking	Your level of consciousness in your waking hours, when you are fully awake and aware of your surrounding environment, feelings, thoughts and perceptions.
Dreaming	Dreaming is our stage of sleep with thoughts, memories and dreams, where we access our subconscious mind.
Deep sleep	It is during this sleeping state of consciousness that we no longer have perceptual or cognitive experiences.
Transcendental consciousness	The pure state where our mind becomes silent but our consciousness is fully awake, and bridges to other states of deeper consciousness.
Cosmic consciousness	Also known as Higher, Divine, or Witness consciousness, cosmic consciousness is achieved when connecting to our pure self and soul, like in the deeply hypnotic therapy of life between life. It is in this consciousness state that we are believed to lose our fear of death.
Glorified state of cosmic consciousness	Also known as refined cosmic consciousness or God consciousness. Defined as a steady flow of pure and unconditional love where perceptions are heightened.

Unified state of cosmic consciousness	Also known as unity consciousness, is where we are infinite and beyond our sense of pure self.
	It is in this state that we reach a realisation that we are united, there is a oneness, with everything all around us, and that we all come from pure source, and ultimately, we will all return Home to source when our earthly incarnation ends.

Soul

Whilst our consciousness changes throughout our days and incarnations, the soul is more consistent and is a permanent entity. It is said that nothing lasts forever, but our soul may just be the one exception to this adage. Our soul is the spiritual part of our human existence which is immortal and brings life force to our physical body. The brain is accountable for reason, thinking, perception, and memory, but it is the soul that stores these teachings beyond the life you have now.

It could be proffered that one of the reasons society fears death so much is because we view the soul as being separate from our body. We all have souls; we all are souls. Each and every one of us is born with a life purpose which we will endeavour to fulfil during each incarnation. The soul incorporates our connection to a divine power, whether you know this as Source, the Creator, God, Goddess, Father Sky, Great Spirit, or other respected term. It is because of this divine connection that we come to be more powerful than we realise and why we are never truly alone.

As well as our inner soul, there are other connections that ensure we are never alone. Have you ever had one of those initial encounters, where you think, "Have I met you before?" or you have instantly felt a connection or a dislike to someone, often before they even mutter a word? They are probably members of your Soul Family, or Soul Group as it is also known.

Members of our soul family can comprise of an individual or a group of people who resonate with us on an energetic and subconscious level at a moment in time. The bond that follows transcends through time and dimensions, where they have been cut from the same energetic material as yourself. These connections can be blissful, challenging, platonic or romantic, serving the purpose of helping you experience the life lessons your soul needs to experience in this particular incarnation. Other terms such as "twin flame" and "soulmate" are used to describe intense romantic connections. However, it should be noted that the path of true love may not run smoothly for you, as there may be lessons to be learned, and so challenges may be presented, as this is from where our greatest growth comes.

You may be aware of terms such as "your soul's purpose", which is all about why you are on this earth at this time, what life lessons you are here to learn, and how you can shine your unique light in the world. Your soul does not experience its greatest growth through a happy and trouble-free relationship or sitting cross-legged on a yoga mat and chanting "om". It will experience its greatest expansion through more trying times, such as experiencing death and loss, where we are tested beyond any challenge that we had previously faced or overcome. The soul, just like life itself, does not come with an instruction manual, but there are ways in which you can access it more deeply. This includes listening to your intuition, partaking in activities you love, meditation, and other pastimes that affect our brainwaves.

Elisabeth Kübler-Ross is best known for her five stages of grief, but she also wrote extensively on the subject of life after death. She once wrote, "consciously or not, we are all on the quest for answers, trying to learn the lessons of life," and we truly are. We search for purpose, meaning, love, and power, whilst grappling with fear, loss, guilt, worthiness, and time. It is through modalities such as past life regression that we can start to discover the answers to our ongoing search and questioning about our life.

Past Life Regression

Past Life Regression (PLR) is a branch of hypnotherapy, which is used to access past lives, and the memories and experiences within these previous incarnations. It is not essential that the client believes in spirituality or reincarnation to undergo the therapeutic process of past life regression. The aims and benefit of this is usually to pursue a psychotherapeutic or spiritual experience, heal relationships, fears, phobias, and illness, as well as clearing any vows, oaths, or curses that may be inhibiting one's greatest potential in their current life.

The hypnotherapist will use various tools and techniques to safely direct the client back to their earliest memory of the current life issue, often through connecting with the residual energy or keywords that are subconsciously associated with the past.

Through research and working with my own past life regression clients, I have discovered how the body remembers as much as the mind. It appears that when we experience an emotional upset or trauma in our life, we will create both a physical and emotional memory of the event. Body psychotherapy is an entire modality in itself, which is a psychotherapy approach to the mind and body connection. In brief, indicators for physical manifestations of both physical or emotional trauma can be seen in past lives and current lives, often recurring when they are not addressed and resolved. We speak subconsciously of such blocks when we say about "the weight of the world on our shoulders" or "I don't have the guts to do that" or we experience idiopathic health issues in this life.

Throughout life, most of us will experience some level of trauma. Similarly to those moments preceding death where the soul can leave the physical body prior to the event, our body has a self-defence mechanism, whereby we can dissociate at the onset of trauma. In times of abuse, rape, and accidents, we can fragment and dissociate from our body, generally through the left-hand side of our physical body. I have seen this many times in my regression clients, where people will say prior to the session "it was like a part of me died that day" or "I have always felt like something is missing from me since that event" and then there are many scientifically-proven accounts of out of body experiences and near death experiences.

By undergoing PLR we can witness and form a greater understanding of the continuum of life, as we revisit our death point in a previous life, and so know that we will inevitably come back. PLR has so many positive attributes, such as removing mental blocks and fears in our current life, some of which is the fear of dying. The reason I chose to include PLR in this grief guidebook is that I have noted over the years how clients had come to me due to severe and unrelenting grief, and would inevitably come to discover that the emotional resonance was linked to a past life. Many clients had been with their estranged or deceased loved one in a former life, and had either made a vow to never love anyone else ever again, or had been so heartbroken in a previous life and was now experiencing the same emotional resonance in this life. It was if their grief encounter was doubled due to the past life loss and the one in their current reality.

Whilst PLR may seem controversial or inappropriate in a practical grief guidebook, I do not believe that there is any one way for grief recovery, and endeavour to provide an eclectic blend of tools and suggestions, to help each and every one of you. Whilst some of you will be drawn to conventional talking therapies, others may feel curious to try something new and unknown just like their grief path is. What I will say is that PLR works well during times of heightened and raw emotions, so you do not have to be coping well with your grief to commence regression sessions.

Life Between Life

As we discussed in earlier chapters, Life Between Life (LBL) is our soul's existence between incarnations. As we learned from the definitions of the soul, the soul is on an immortal journey, and just one stage of its journey is LBL or Interlife Regression.

This deeply hypnotic experience differs from PLR, not only in the depth of the hypnotic state, but in how LBL is only concerned with the soul's journey in the stage between your immediate past life and your current incarnation. LBL can address specific objectives that are pertaining to where you are right now. Key questions are often related to life purpose, choosing the right path ahead, life lessons that need to be learned, and looking at the life choices such as culture and soul members. It is in LBL that you may come to be aware of why your recent loss occurred, from a soul perspective, as it may well be pertaining to your loved one's life lessons as well as your own.

Beyond the humanistic questions, LBL offers the opportunity to investigate your spirituality, looking into how many incarnations you have had, discovering your soul name, and discovering which creative or spiritual tools to develop or enhance for your soul's highest purpose in this life.

Future Life Progression

As the title suggests, Future Life Progression (FLP) is a waking dream state that can be accessed through both hypnosis or meditation, to provide a glimpse of your future beyond your current thoughts, dreams, plans and mindset. FLP differs from PLR in that it is all forward-thinking, as opposed to PLR which concentrates on personal events in your current life or past lives. FLP takes you forward to a place where you can explore the possibilities that extend from your own current mindset, providing you with a wealth of insight and knowledge that would otherwise be unknown to you, and may work well in increasing your hope and drive for your life after loss. FLP can be used to look forward in your current life, but also into a journey into the next life or future lives.

I would personally recommend that you experience guided meditation or hypnosis into your current life or a past life, prior to undergoing FLP. I voice this as you will need to learn and recognise how the information is personally presented to you, be it through a sense of knowing or visualisation. If you are unaware of how your subconscious mind presents information to you, and you undertake FLP and receive no vision of the years ahead, I would hate for you to fear the worse, when in reality it may just be that you are not relaxed enough or are not a visual person.

Current Life Regression

Current Life Regression (CLR) is not greatly different to PLR as both processes are accessed by the same means. Even from the soul's perspective, there is no difference as all regressions form part of the soul's journey and timeline, although obviously there will be no re-encountering of the death point in your current life as you are still very much alive at this point.

CLR can be used to access current life issues, events, emotions, and energies, which may be voiced by the client. However, I have also worked with many clients who have come to me to enable them to access years of their current life where they have no recall of certain periods.

Often, when we revisit past events and unhealed wounds, we will see misconceptions that have become ingrained in our subconscious over the years, and with this new insight and adult perspective, we can finally start to heal, accept, forgive, and move forward with a greater sense of understanding, clarity, and purpose.

It is said that the first seven years of our life are the most important in determining the basis for one's overall success in their life to come. I do not wholeheartedly agree with this idea, as I truly believe that life is what we make of it, and whether you believe you will be a success or a failure, you ultimately will be. However, I do believe that it is during our initial seven years on this earthly plane that we have a time of enhanced learning, as the brain undergoes rapid growth. If something negative occurs during this time, there is often a fear or block that results, and this can come from one singular event or from a repetitive cycle. I have observed how CLR clients will predominantly regress back to the first seven years of their life, where the now-adult version of self will work with their younger self, to see things from a wider perspective, which in turn leads to a great healing, that creates a positive shift and way forward.

Coma (Unconsciousness)

A coma is a prolonged state of deep unconsciousness, whether medically induced or as a result of severe injury or illness. Depending on the cause and extent of damage, a coma can happen rapidly or gradually, and last from hours to years. The main difference between consciousness and unconsciousness is that the comatose are believed to be unaware of self and their external environment, and cannot be awoken by physical stimuli such as noise or pain. Whilst one is unresponsive in a state of unconsciousness, they are not dead, neither physically nor spiritually, but rather in a suspended state. The soul of the person is still believed to be present in the body, but whilst appearing unresponsive to onlookers, consciousness transcends our physical body and can be experiencing Near Death Experiences or Out of Body Experiences whilst in this unconscious condition.

Near Death Experience

As we mentioned earlier, whether we are asleep, awake or dead is all a matter of consciousness. If we are open enough to accept that we are spiritual beings having a physical experience, is it as widely accepted that this allows us to spiritually leave our body and travel to other realms before returning back to the earthly plane and physical body?

A near death experience (NDE) is a profoundly personal experience, which is associated with a moment of perceived impending death from which the soul views the current life from a safe distance, whether this be the earthly plane or beyond.

Just as death is not a recent discovery, neither are near death experiences. NDEs are believed to feature in the Bible, *The Tibetan Book of the Dead*, and in more recent times, the words of Dr Raymond Moody, psychiatrist Elisabeth Kübler-Ross, Dr Eben Alexander, and Dr Penny Sartori.

Whatever your beliefs of such matters are, scientists, medics and a whole plethora of everyday people will have spontaneous moments of spiritual insights, whether or not they choose to recognise them as such. Whilst the world is becoming more open to the subject of NDE, within healthcare, very few practitioners have openness to NDEs, even though patients will speak of a change in awareness and bodily presence during a life-threatening emergency, such as undergoing complicated surgery or a cardiac arrest. Other components include a sense of awareness around having died, a sense of peace or weightlessness, enhanced sensory experiences, a tunnel from darkness to light, meeting deceased loved ones, visiting different realms, future progression, a choice of two or more paths, time distortion, and ineffability.

I have no doubt that NDEs occur and are the epitome of life-changing events, having witnessed my patients' reports and own family members going on to experience many positive life changes. Many years ago, when a patient confided in our team about their personal NDE experience, I was truly fascinated, but I was alone in this. They coyly shared how they viewed from above their body, but their recall was instantly dismissed by the team and reasoned as hypoxia (lack of oxygen), hallucinations from the anaesthetic, or the introduction of new medications.

My own grandmother had an NDE following one of her many trans-ischemic attacks, and no longer feared death or attached importance to material possessions, the opinions of others, or social status. A cousin had an existential crisis which stopped her from taking her own life and went on to help others with mental health issues throughout her career.

Whilst in the main most people who encounter an NDE will go on to experience a positive change in personality and outlook in life, develop psychic abilities, develop healing abilities or become healed, it should be noted that there are always two sides to every story. Whilst NDE provides a positive life change for most, others have struggled to accept the experience, and have presented with negative effects following their NDE, such as post-traumatic stress disorder.

Out of Body Experience

Many believe an out of body experience (OBE) and NDE to be the same thing and use the two terms interchangeably. For the purpose of the book, I proffer that those who have encountered an OBE will report being out of the body, just like in an NDE, however, they tend to only look down from a distance that is still on the earthly plane, and not travelling or visiting beyond earth.

Shared Death Experience

Have you ever had the niggling feeling about a loved one in need, or suddenly awoken in the middle of the night, only to later learn of their passing? Shared Death Experience (SDE), as coined by Dr Raymond Moody, is a relatively new term in society today, although research suggests that it may simply have been a recognised phenomenon back in the late 1800s but known by different terms such as deathbed visitations or deathbed coincidences.

SDE is when we not only share a life with a loved one but their death too. This is not as horrific or as frightening as it may first sound, and can actually be a beautiful and empathic experience, and can occur whether they are in the same space or miles apart.

Regardless of belief, religion, or background, friends and family of the dying have shared how they had heard mystical music, such as angelic voices or harps, playing as death nears. Others tell of a mystical light appearing in the room, at which time many bystanders – myself included – have witnessed a mist, fog, steam, or cloud-like formation emitting from the body of the dying. I have seen this rise up from out of the chest and up towards the head before disappearing, which I always took to be the soul leaving the physical body.

Whilst many people will openly confess of a change in room temperature around the time of dying, far fewer speak of a change in the geometry of the room. The room change is different to many, but in the main, it will shift beyond its four-wall figuration, and may soften or blur, and even feel circular or tunnel-like in its formation. Research into SDEs has reported that the friends and family members have had their own OBE and viewed the imminent death from above the room of the dying, with some experiencing a strong upward pull on their body, witnessing snippets of the afterlife along with the dying person, encountering beings of light, a life review, conversations with other deceased loved ones, and encountering a different realm, areas of which will be discussed later in this book, in the chapter The Afterlife and Life Thereafter.

Whilst sceptics will claim anaesthesia, pharmacology, dehydration, hypoxia or anoxia are causing the patient's alleged hallucinations towards the end of life, there is the unmedicated and perfectly healthy loving bystander who is also part of this same experience which is not as easy to dismiss, and may remain beyond our ability to explain and fully understand.

What we do know from research and a logical standpoint, notably Dr Raymond Moody's research in his book, *Glimpses of Eternity*, is that when the friends and family have experienced an SDE, there is a dramatic reduction in the grief recovery process, as they have experienced first hand that their loved one is actually alive and well in the afterlife, simply in a new level of consciousness. Such sacred insight can aid in reducing fears around death, and indeed provide a new depth of understanding of one's own life more.

Grief

There is no fundamental and proven process on how we should grieve, although many people will attempt to bestow their personal experience and wisdom on us. Grief is like our fingerprints; unique to us and not like anyone else's. If grief really is unique for each individual, can grief be overcome? Is grief curable? My heart cannot speak for yours, but I do believe that the best cure for grief is to grieve.

In this chapter we will deeply explore the subject of the different grieving processes, but before we do this, let us look at the basic terms that are used when discussing the subject of grief.

Grief, Bereavement or Mourning?

Grief, bereavement, and mourning are often terms that are used interchangeably in order to describe the reaction to death of a loved one, but they actually have slightly different meanings. To me, bereavement and mourning fall under the umbrella term of grief, and as such are part of how we experience grief as a whole.

Grief is a completely normal reaction to the loss of someone, but it can also be a reaction to the loss of connection to a certain area of our life: be it a relationship, health, physical ability, finances, opportunities, or future hopes and dreams.

Bereavement is a type of grief, an emotional state of being that singularly follows having experienced the death of a loved one. It is the time after the death, during which grief is experienced, and when mourning then occurs.

Mourning is an external expression of grief. It tends to go beyond the individual's natural emotions and is often strongly influenced by a person's religious and cultural beliefs. Complex cultural behaviours tend to dictate how and when mourning should be expressed. For example, Catholicism believes spouses should mourn for a year and a day, in China close relatives should grieve for one hundred days, Buddhists say ninety days, and Sikhism requires a ten-day mourning period.

By way of contrast, others celebrate the life of the deceased, such as the Irish with the merry wake, New Orleans with their jazz funerals, and the Nyakyusa of Tanzania dancing and flirting at funerals. Although the method of mourning differs between various countries and belief systems, there is one universal theme, and that is that honouring the deceased is prevalent in all who mourn.

Throughout this book I tend to use the term grief rather than bereavement or mourning, as I discuss both loss (also known as mini deaths) and death itself. As such, the word grief is an all-encompassing term to cover bereavement, mourning, and a multitude of other experiences that are part of grief.

What is Grief?

Grief cannot be defined in one simple sentence, as grief itself is not simple. It is a vast and complex topic with equally vast and complex presentations in terms of signs and symptoms, longevity, and intensity. Grief is one of the most uncomfortable subjects of discussion, and if you are grieving you may struggle with expressing what is happening to you. As an onlooker, there may be an awkwardness, avoidance, or silence in the presence of the griever. Despite what may be perceived as abnormal behaviours, grief is a completely normal and natural reaction to loss, yet it is one of the most misunderstood experiences in our lives.

Grief, along with death, is still a relatively taboo subject in a world where, despite rallying for free speech, and social media seeing us airing what would have previously been our best guarded thoughts, our grief still tends to be hushed. Keeping our grief within us can have profound negative effects on our well-being, as when we feel unable to air our thoughts and feelings, which can leave us feeling emotionally incomplete or unable to seek closure around our life-changing loss.

For as long as there has been human emotion, there has been grief. However, like life itself, everything changes over time, and this includes the ways in which we grieve. I like to think of grief as a journey rather than a final destination. As with any journey, we do not stay in one place, we keep moving forward through different areas, which in the case of grief can be anything from sadness through to enlightenment.

The grief journey is varied in its milestones, depending on a wide variety of factors: the nature of death (expected or unexpected), our relationship with the deceased (sibling, parent, or the relationship being close or estranged), our personality, resilience and coping mechanisms, previous life experiences, support networks (family, friends, social communities and connection to ourselves), and cultural, spiritual and religious beliefs.

When Grief Strikes

When death occurs, it will be hard to listen to the words that this event is only the end of a chapter of our life rather than the conclusion of our entire life story. We may be feeling that our own life is a fragile mirror that has suddenly been dropped and shattered into a million pieces and is no longer of any great consequence or purpose. However, as our life journey will continue, and as we start to piece all of those shattered fragments back together, we will begin to see the whole picture once again. There may be fine cracks running throughout, but allow yourself to imagine that it is through these small fissures that we will enable a glimmer of light to shine back into our life.

I am here to reassure you that you will get through this experience of loss and death, the madness, the numbness, and other exacerbations, as it is all part of the healing process that we have labelled as grief. As part of the inevitable changes from your experience of grief, you will have to navigate your way through the emotions that will swing like a pendulum, with your thoughts swaying from one extreme to another. You will not know all the answers, never mind how long and hard you search for them, and sometimes – just to add to your feelings of confusion and uncertainty – it will seem like you have too many choices and an overwhelming abundance of possible answers.

Grief is a natural response and process that we must endure to reach a new stage in our life. It can lead us to a place of growth, awakening and profound healing; provided we embrace the lessons it offers to teach us.

The Grief Process

Despite the negative portrayal of grief, the grieving process holds a positive internal experience and purpose that lends itself to a time of recovery and self-discovery. Our grief can take us from our previously hurried daily existence to a slower reality; one that allows us to "be in the now" or even stop us altogether, which may be for the first time in years. We may start to look at things differently, as everything we had previously observed, trusted and understood to be a certainty has now changed. This shift can lead us to truly question all aspects of our life, whilst noting the deficits between what was, what is, and what it is we wish for in our future.

We may develop greater self-awareness, and can even discover we are stronger and more resilient than we were ever told or managed to realise for ourselves. Our sadness will mirror what is actually important to us in our life, and whilst our life may look like a shattered mirror beyond repair, the slowing of energy enables us to discover potential ways to start piecing our life back together in the best possible way.

Throughout my years in Haematology and Oncology nursing, I came to see the change in people that occurs following a life-altering diagnosis which I referred to as BC and AD: Before Cancer and After Diagnosis. When patients heard their cancer diagnosis, many would experience grief from the losses cancer would bring: loss of health, image, confidence, finances, control, and known way of life. However, whilst science can predict trajectories of such an illness, it cannot measure the power of the human spirit. Whilst some were brought to their knees upon hearing of their cancer, many patients would stand tall and see their diagnosis as an awakening; a calling to find a greater meaning in life, a second chance, or a moment of clarity where they finally understood what was truly important in life. Regardless of whether our grief reaction to a life-changing event is perceived as negative or positive, grief certainly teaches us about purpose and meaning, even though we may not recognise this life lesson at the time.

Kübler-Ross postulated that there are five key emotions experienced by terminally ill patients prior to death. As a student nurse, I remember creating the acronym DABDA, to remind me of those stages: Denial, Anger, Bargaining, Depression and Acceptance. Realistically, grief goes beyond the model of five simplistic stages and can often look like a dropped bowl of tangled spaghetti with emotions all over the place. For others, it can be a simple and straight path of new beginnings and positivity. I have seen more waves and loops of grief than I have stages, but whether you grieve in a subconscious uniformity or in peaks and troughs, one thing that you must do is to give yourself permission to go through the grieving process.

Ignoring or suppressing grief will only defer the inevitable further along our timeline; for true healing to commence, it is necessary to recognise and actively engage with grief. It is like when a young child is repeatedly calling "Mum, Mum, Mum, Mum, Mum, Mum, Mum" like an unrelenting bleating lamb. We know it is there and vying for our attention, but despite our best efforts to ignore the matter at hand, it will eventually overcome us. That which is not acknowledged cannot be changed; whether it be our busy thoughts during meditation, an unfulfilled dream that keeps twanging at our heartstrings, or those trapped tears that need to flow. Acknowledge your grief and allow your unique authenticity to flow, be they tears of relief or sorrow.

Did you know that crying is actually good for you? Far better than "putting on a brave face" crying is a therapeutic self-healing process. When we cry for long periods of time, we release oxytocin and endorphins (our happy chemicals) which ease both our physical and emotional pain. It is a beautiful self-soothing action that already exists within us as a human being. Everything you need is already within you. Why put on a brave face, when you could wear a tear-stained face that is embarking on a healing journey?

Signs and Symptoms of Grief

Whilst experiencing the death of a loved one may not kill us, we can be left feeling as if something within us has died. It may feel like someone, or something, has screwed up our blueprint for life, causing us to temporarily lose sight of our way ahead. It is during these unsettling times that we develop the greatest sense of belief, that we will rediscover ourselves and life direction.

It should be noted that grief may not always be due to a loss of a loved one. What expressions of grief do we experience when we lose someone with whom we shared a different connection? An absent parent. The abusive partner. An unloved one. A partner for whom illness turned them into our patient. A parent who no longer recognises us. In such cases, we may not just experience emotions such as sadness and despair, but rather relief; be it for the sufferer from their illness or ourselves as we are released from a dutiful way of life. All grief will inevitably lead us to a different way forward, but for some, it may feel more optimistic, like a new lease of life rather than a conscious effort to forge a new way forward.

Heightened emotions will prevail for many, and some of those emotions will be so closely related, it may be hard to know which is which, and how you are authentically feeling in the moment. Are you angry or fearful? Full of love or pure grief? It can often be hard to differentiate as when we come face to face with adversity our brain tends to activate an adrenaline-fuelled "fight-or-flight" response. This physiological occurrence causes our brain to be in a state of heightened awareness, and our body becomes poised and ready for action. This natural reaction is ultimately an unnecessary process for the situation we find ourselves in, as there is not actually anywhere for us to go, or anything for us to do. Being in this state with no way of direct action to take to resolve our fight-or-flight response will have a negative impact on our overall physical, emotional, mental, and behavioural processes. These can present in several ways:

Physical

Headaches, migraines, dizziness, rashes, skin changes (eczema, psoriasis, hives), skin sensitivity, weakened immune system (colds, viruses, shingles), sore throat, dry mouth, insomnia, flu-like symptoms, digestion problems, loss of appetite, binge eating, tiredness, fatigue, aching, physical pain, sickness, nausea, diarrhoea, constipation, palpitations, impotence, sweating, shivering, clamminess, visual disturbances, menstrual disturbances (missed periods, heightened premenstrual syndrome symptoms), increased blood pressure, heart palpitations, chest pains, change to breathing patterns, shortness of breath, increased sensitivity to noise and light.

Emotional

Sadness, anger, disbelief, despair, guilt, raw, numbness, loneliness, emptiness, pained, denial, bargaining, acceptance, regret, confusion, uncertain, shame, detached, hysteria, grace, resentful, relieved, searching, yearning, tearful, crying.

Mental

Forgetfulness, lack of concentration, confusion, poor memory, low mood, depression, suicidal ideation, negative thoughts, anxiety, panic attacks, overthinking, questioning previous life choices (religion, career, relationships).

Behavioural

Altered sleep patterns, dreams, nightmares, flashbacks, jumpiness, paranoia, defensiveness, memory lapses, panic attacks, loss of appetite, overeating, increased alcohol consumption, impulsive or rebellious choices, inertia, noise sensitivity, hyperactivity, lack of motivation or interest, disconnecting from people around you, or unusual emotional reactions to normal situations, questioning spiritual and religious beliefs.

Social

Some friends may avoid you because they don't know what to say or how to help you in your grief journey. You may feel pressure to appear strong for friends or family members, or choose to withdraw and be alone in isolation due to heightened emotions.

Spiritual

Loss of faith, religion, spirituality, purpose or meaning in life, a new search for faith, religion, spirituality or meaning in life, spiritual emergence, praying, superstition, questioning or strengthening long-held beliefs.

Whilst the physical, emotional, mental, behavioural, social and spiritual signs and symptoms are temporary occurrences, they can impact on us, which leads us to a greater need to find ways in which to recover and move forward from the death and its subsequent grief process. But how easy is it? And how long does grief and its plethora of symptoms last?

Grief Recovery Time

I am sorry to say that there is no timetable or checklist on grief that I can share with you. Every loss, whether from a way of life or a death, will trigger a grief reaction, which can vary from sheer relief to absolute despair.

The bereaved will often speak of The Seasons of Grief, in which they refer to the experience of having to go through an entire year and its four seasons before they truly start to overcome grief. In those seasons, we will come face to face with memories of birthdays, anniversaries, seasonal celebrations, and personal days, with a true sense of awareness that it is for the first time without a loved one by our side, which can trigger a nostalgic stream of thoughts on what could have, should have and would have been.

How long should it take one to grieve? It is a rather strange question and may even be perceived as offensive. But grief is a process and processes tend to have a time range in which certain stages occur, right? In this case, this would be wrong. Whilst Mother Nature or chemical reactions may well work in a timely fashion, but when we are dealing with one's own unique personalities, coping strategies, beliefs, and more, there is no clear-cut timeframe within which to work in times of grieving.

Is speeding up the grief process disrespectful? Is a practical guide to quicken grief recovery inappropriate? No, not according to recent research, and the reality that our life goes on, so why not ease our grief symptoms so that we can be more present in our life? George A. Bonanno, a professor of clinical psychology, has undertaken extensive research showing how grief can be approached differently, and even mentions joy, in his book *The Other Side of Sadness: What the New Science of Bereavement Tells Us About Life After Loss*.

In terms of grief in the death of our loved ones, our

beloved departed are moving on with their own next level of consciousness and lessons beyond this earthly plane, and we too must endeavour to move on with our own life and its lessons that await us. This doesn't mean forgetting them or superseding their existence, but moreover, striving to create our best life thereafter. We must find a path that prevents us from making one chapter in our life the one thing that defines our entire life story. We must endeavour to search for the lesson in the loss, grieve the life-changing event, and trust ourselves enough to become the hero in our own unique journey.

Whether we have been struck by a death or a mini death, grief will undoubtedly follow, but we may not always recognise it at the time. Why not? Because grief may not even be there at the time of loss. There are numerous ways in which the human mind will lead us into grief, so we shall now look at the different forms that grief takes.

Types of Grief

Back in the early 2000s when I was studying my nursing degree, we touched on grief, and the basic meaning of the term. Given how much death occurs in the arena of healthcare, a dictionary definition and short group discussion of what we understood by the word "grief" was completely insufficient for our line of work. We would naturally come face to face with grieving family members, and would often feel inadequate with our words of comfort, or helping them to understand what to expect in the forthcoming days, weeks, and months ahead.

Fast forward twenty years and the definitions and understanding of the subject of grief has expanded to cover a broader range of types, starting from what is labelled as Normal Grief through to Pandemic Grief.

Normal Grief (Common Grief)

Contrary to what the name might suggest, there really are no set guidelines to define normal grief in terms of timelines, emotions or severity. Instead, think of normal grief as any response that ticks the boxes of grief in a predictable manner.

Normal grief is a temporary state where the intensity of grief will naturally dissipate over time. As one shows the ability to move towards accepting their loss, the emotional intensity gradually decreases, whilst the ability to undertake basic daily activities and normal routines remain, despite grief symptoms simmering under the surface. It's both normal and common for acute outbursts of emotions as our grief catches us unaware, but the intensity of these sporadic behaviours will lessen over time as we come to adjust to life after loss. As individuals develop a new sense of self and their surroundings, they often speak of a new normal, as they experience a new way of life following their loss.

Anticipatory Grief

Grief is something we believe happens after a death, but with anticipatory grief, it happens before death arrives, carrying symptoms of normal grief with it. Emotions such as anger and sadness may be experienced, often with exhaustion from being a carer, or from feeling overwhelmed by the reality that lies ahead. Anticipatory grief is relatively new and unknown in terms of the overall process of grief, and is seen when there is a known pending death as a result of a long-term illness or rapid deterioration of health. As family members understand and accept the inevitable end, their grieving process may begin.

Anticipatory grief can be one of confusion, as the loved one is still very much physically present, and yet the mind and emotions are in a place of both a current and future reality. It is in anticipatory grief that we may observe Kübler-Ross's five stages occurring: denial, anger, bargaining, depression, and acceptance.

Ambiguous Grief (Living Grief)

Ambiguous grief – sometimes referred to as living grief – is not always recognised as a form of grief when we are experiencing it, and instead it may be misdiagnosed as depression or post-traumatic stress disorder.

Ambiguous grief is a grieving that occurs without a physical death, which can present in two ways. One is where there is a physical absence but a psychological presence such as a relationship breakdown or someone away on military service. The other presentation is the reverse, where there is a psychological absence but physical presence, which we may experience with those with a life-limiting illness or diagnosis, dementia, traumatic brain injury, or being in a coma.

Unlike a physical death, ambiguous losses can cause the individual to become stuck within the grieving process, as there is no recognised death, funeral, or healing process to attach the grief to, as certain aspects of living still remain. It is as if the griever's emotions are as ambiguous as the title itself. Ambiguous grief can lead to times of confusion, when left without closure or clear understanding of the loss. As we search for answers or begin to grieve the potential future loss, the normal grief process can become triggered or even delayed as we become entwined with our emotions, a search for answers and trying to plan a practical way forward.

Complicated Grief

Defining complicated grief is indeed a complicated task. Many define complicated grief as an umbrella that covers traumatic, prolonged, delayed and distorted grief, and you may even see it referred to as chronic, or pathological grief. For ease of definition, and because grief is so unique and individualised, I have separated out traumatic, prolonged, delayed and distorted grief as I believe there to be notable differences between them.

Complicated grief refers to normal grief that becomes severe in longevity and significantly impairs the ability to function. It can be difficult to judge when grief has lasted too long, as grief is without timeframes. However, it is generally understood that complicated grief is when debilitating grief is unrelenting and continues for over six months. Signs of complicated grief are when the griever no longer believes they have a sense of identity without the deceased and often feel that they cannot function alone. Complicated grief is commonly seen in people who have lost their long-time partner, and will often be hopelessly searching and yearning for their loved one. Characteristics of this grief include irrational thoughts, and feeling of being emotionally trapped with no positive way forward or a conducive end in sight.

In complicated grief, where the grief does not naturally abate after six months, healthcare professional intervention may be both appropriate and effective. Without intervention, grief symptoms can further develop into a decline in mental health, or exacerbate pre-existing mental health conditions, like depression, anxiety or post-traumatic stress disorder.

Other contributing factors in diagnosing complicated grief include the nature of the loss or death, the relationship to the deceased, genetics, personality, and their environment. Warning signs to be mindful of as a supporter are when someone is experiencing self-destructive behaviour, deep and persistent feelings of guilt, low self-esteem, suicidal talk, thoughts or attempts, violent outbursts, or radical lifestyle changes. Healthcare professionals now recognise complicated grief to be more of a disorder than a non-medical condition, and now prescribe – whether pharmaceutical or social – therapies and treatments for chronic grief symptoms.

Traumatic Grief

When there is a tragedy at the heart of the loss – a sudden and unexpected death – one can expect to see a traumatic grief.

There are more presentations than the normal grief process, as there are additional layers of trauma, which can cause fear, anxiety, anger, change, or self-reproach. Traumatic grief can be triggered in unexpected, sudden deaths, such as the death of a child, a road traffic accident, or a terrorist attack.

Prolonged Grief

Similar to complicated grief, prolonged grief does not only cover a longer period of time, but is intense. This grief presents itself as one becoming so incapacitated by the grief, their activities of daily living are impaired over the long term. One may also be struggling greatly without the loved ones and other forms of loss, which leads them to lingering over their past, the death itself, and with a longing to be reunited with the deceased individual.

Delayed Grief

Delayed grief is when reactions and emotions in response to a death are postponed until a later time, be it a conscious or subconscious action. When grief is delayed, there is no timeframe as to when the cloak of sadness will come to engulf us. It may be that we are busy and practical in the initial days following the death; dealing with the funeral arrangements and conversing with the vast presence of people being around means that we have no time or space to process the reality of our recent void. However, as bystanders inevitably return to their own life, the vacant space in the life of the griever creates a stillness where we then start to reflect on our loss.

Delayed grief may occur years – or even lifetimes – after a loss, triggered by another event that may initially appear totally unrelated. Grief reactions may appear excessive to the current reality, so whilst in the current day there may have been a loss of a job, house or health, the replicated emotions will bring about residual unresolved grief from a past loss. I have witnessed this repeatedly with both my nursing and regression clients, where I will ask them when they last felt this specific emotion, and direct them back to the original source of the emotion, which will lead them to an early loss in this life or even a past life. When delayed grief appears, it will feel like normal grief but often comes out of nowhere. This should be a welcome appearance, enabling us to start releasing our grief from both the past and the present.

Distorted Grief

Distorted grief is where the griever can become stuck in one stage of grief. In distorted grief, one is stuck in the anger stage of grief, where they are angry at themselves, others, the deceased, and the world at large. Whilst it is a normal reaction and emotion to be angered at a death or the deceased, extreme and prolonged changes in behaviour, both to oneself and others, goes beyond the parameters of normal grief.

Disenfranchised Grief

In a nutshell, disenfranchised grief is when grief is not socially recognised or acknowledged. This has to be one of the saddest forms of grief which can leave the griever feeling invalidated or insignificant, due to their family, community or culture. Onlookers may not understand the importance or the significance of the loss, for example, loss of a pet, a co-worker, or miscarriage, or where the death is stigmatised, such as drunk driving, an extramarital affair, or an ex-partner. The griever can often feel uncertain of their emotions and become entangled with questioning, and the current reality. It is due to the lack of clarity around disenfranchised grief that it is sometimes also referred to or compared to ambiguous grief.

At times, people with disenfranchised grief can experience intensified grief symptoms, often triggered by lack of social support. If left untreated, disenfranchised grief can develop into severe clinical depression, suicidal thoughts or attempts, and substance abuse, similar to the presentations seen with complicated grief.

Cumulative Grief

Cumulative grief has been known as "grief overload" or Secondary Loss Grief and occurs when one experiences a second loss when they are still grieving a separate, initial loss. This type of grief can occur when multiple losses are experienced, often within a short period of time, and it can start with one life-changing event. The secondary losses are closely related to the first loss, so when a loved one dies, we also experience the second level of grief through loss of companionship, loss of income and daily routine. It is as you begin to attempt to return to your known way of life, that the secondary grief rises, as you experience eating alone, and maintaining the home by yourself.

I have witnessed healthcare professionals present with signs and symptoms of cumulative grief, when they have had no sacred time or opportunity to adequately grieve for a patient who has died, before the next patient is brought into the environment for their care, which over time can lead to emotional exhaustion and burnout.

Masked Grief

Masked grief is where the grief affects the physical body and behaviour in ways that impair normal daily activities, but the griever is unaware and unable to recognise the link between their physical ailments and behaviour with their grief. Masked grief is invisible grief which commonly affects men, children, cultures or society, often when they are dictated how to grieve or not grieve, based on their informant's own grief experiences or rulings. This suppressed grief reaction can lead to delayed grief or more complex grief can occur at a later date.

Exaggerated Grief

Exaggerated grief is where the griever becomes so overwhelmed by the death of their loved one, that they develop major psychiatric disorders such as fears and phobias, suicidal ideation, self-destructive behaviour, nightmares and disabling helplessness. Exaggerated grief is concerned with a severe inability to function in our day-to-day activities and for a prolonged length of time, with a tendency to regress with their grief rather than move forward. Healthcare professional intervention is needed in these cases.

Inhibited Grief

Inhibited grief can be defined in a couple of ways. Sometimes it may appear that a griever is purposely avoiding the reality of losing something or someone by turning their attention to distractions in life as to avoid their new reality. However, inhibited grief can also describe someone who does not openly display their signs of grief, consciously choosing to keep them private. Like any unresolved grief, it tends to lead to delayed or more intense grief at a later time in life.

Collective Grief

Collective grief is felt by a group, be it a community, society or a nation, as a result of a natural disaster, death of a public figure, or a terrorist attack.

Abbreviated Grief

Abbreviated grief is a short-lived response to a loss, but a genuine grief form nonetheless. Abbreviated grief is seen when the grieving process appears to be worked through quicker than what is perceived to be normal. This could occur due to someone or something immediately filling the void (a new relationship), a minimal emotional connection to the deceased (a distant relative or absent parent), a positive mindset towards life after loss, or the experience of anticipatory grief (such as in life-limiting illness).

Throughout my nursing career, I came to know and love the power of the individual mind. How two people could be dealt a life-changing diagnosis, yet one would embrace absolute strength and the mindset to overcome the illness, whilst another would resign themselves to a death sentence and hand all their power and decisions over to the medical team. It is through this observation that I have formed a real connection with the abbreviated form of grief. When we lose something or someone in life, some of us will choose to meander around in our nostalgic thoughts, questioning, and a negative mindset, while the other will shrug off the experience, embrace the lesson, and will be looking to welcome their next challenging experience. Abbreviated grief is not a lesser grief, just a more rapid recovery.

Absent Grief

Absent grief is often defined as there being no signs of grief following a death, which can often be the case when there has been anticipatory grief prior to the death. It is, however, important to note that in some instances, just because you can't see the signs of grief, it doesn't necessarily mean that someone is not grieving. Be kind to yourself and others, always.

Pandemic Grief

We are rarely ever prepared for death and grief during "normal" times, but the pandemic which struck the world in 2020 created a new perspective on the fragile line between life and death. There was a notable shift from feeling immortal, particularly among the young and healthy, into everyone facing the reality that there are limits on how and when we live and die.

The Coronavirus (COVID-19) pandemic revealed a new type of grief, one which is multifaceted in its presentations.

Firstly, as the health of our loved ones deteriorated within the hospital settings, they were declining without us by their side. The anger, guilt, questioning, and sadness that came from this loss of control and hopelessness triggered a grief response in many. And then the second layer of grief hits: death itself, and once again, without us being allowed to be present.

The third aspect of pandemic grief came from COVID-19 survivors who spoke of how they themselves experienced an overwhelming sense of grief during their illness. Not simply from their loss of health and certainty, but intense emotions such as despair, sadness, hopelessness, and depression.

The fourth part of pandemic grief was the loss of normalcy, when the government placed us in lockdown so we were unable to go about our usual day of work, to socialise as we would have done before, to have a reliable income, or to freely travel, leading to nations grieving the loss of the life we knew and trusted. The four layers of grief and the emotional impact of COVID-19 created huge repercussions and grief symptoms for many months and years ahead.

Grief Styles

As we have seen through the different types of grief, some categories overlap or sound the same, which can add even more confusion and uncertainty into our mind about the grief process. The ever-changing boundaries of death and the subsequent grief can make it difficult to know whether you are grieving, how you are grieving, and subsequently, how to recover from the grief within.

However, whilst the types of grief are vast, the styles in which we grieve tend to fall into just two categories: instrumental and intuitive grieving.

The instrumental grieving style places an emphasis on physical and cognitive tasks, which help control or minimise our emotional expressions of grief. Whereas, by way of contrast, intuitive grieving heightens the emotional experience, riding the waves of emotions through sharing thoughts and feelings, and exploring the loss and their own mortality. Intuitive grievers are more likely to seek and accept support, through self-help groups or conventional talking therapies.

The two extremes of instrumental and intuitive grieving often lend themselves to be merged as one undergoes grief recovery. When this emergence occurs, it is known as blended grief. This seems a natural occurrence, given how emotions and perceptions change as we adjust to our loss. Grief recovery will be discussed further in The Grief Toolbox chapter, but for now, let us look at our loved one's journey as well as our own, in the next chapter, Afterlife, and Life Thereafter.

Afterlife

Your heart, mind and belief system may not be ready to accept that death is not the end of the journey, merely a change in our consciousness, so I will keep it simple with a brief overview of what the afterlife is all about.

Definitions of the Afterlife

Different religions hold various beliefs on what happens to us upon our death, but discussing each and every religion is not the purpose of this book. In the main, the term "afterlife" is used to describe the state of being following one's death; a transition from one home to another. Through a plethora of religions and belief systems, the afterlife is referred to by many names, from A for Arcadia to Z for Zion, including Heaven, Nirvana, immortality, the Promised Land, paradise, and the afterworld. Whilst each religion and set of beliefs will differ, many a notion is that when someone dies and leaves their physical existence here on earth, their soul continues its journey on to a more elevated and enlightened plane of existence.

Our beliefs regarding religion and spirituality construct our thoughts around the soul's journey and are intensely personal to us, with your current reality being a reflection of your strongest belief systems. What we believe happens to the soul upon our physical death can heavily inform our subsequent grief response. As such, a deep exploration of how we feel about the nature of the soul and the afterlife can help us put our loss into a personal perspective. Without this, grief and its many questions may linger and be prolonged, impeding our ability to carry on.

My personal belief is that our soul will continually reincarnate and evolve, and that there is an afterlife; a divine realm, where we meet with a wise consulate and look back on each immediate past incarnation and assess the life lessons. A realm of love, no matter what your life experience was, as I personally do not believe there is any such place as hell. We have the tendency to create our own idea of hell, when our human mind thinks we will be punished for our choices, actions or inactions during this earthly incarnation. However, at the end of our days, I believe we are heading home to a restorative place of love and reflection. The all-seeing God, Universe, or other respected terms, are incapable, and unwilling, to create a place of hurt, hatred or judgement. We come to earth for our own unique karma, life lessons and evolution. We do not have good, bad, right or wrong experiences, just experiences with which to return home and evaluate, before evolving to our next level. There can be a figurative hell on earth at times, be it war, conflict, trauma, deterioration of health, or other life challenges, but at the end of your earthly incarnation days, the hell ends and you go home to heal.

Some regression clients, when experiencing their death point in a previous incarnation, have told of travelling through tunnels or open space with a great resistance due to imagery of snarling faces, grasping hands, or a floor of flames. However, when instructed to investigate this imagery from a sensory aspect, so to focus on what they are feeling rather than on what they are thinking, the deeper insight reveals it is their premeditated expectations of what they are expecting to see, when actually, the true path home is smoother, straighter, and more welcoming. We can be guilty of adopting a negative mindset and proffered outcome in this life when we expect people to treat or respond to us negatively due to our life choices, actions and inactions, but in reality, our fears never come to fruition here on earth, so they will most certainly not come into fruition in the higher state of the afterlife when there is no ego, only pure love.

It may be of interest to note that, from my personal experience, all the negative transitions through hellish passages in regression clients have come from those who have just tapped into a past life where they have experienced life lessons as a perpetrator; the abuser, the murderer, the unfaithful lover, the traitor to their country. As they exist in a past life of perceived wrongdoings, they start to fear and expect the worst with their logical mind, and this is purely their concept of self. Whilst the logical human mind will battle with perceptions of how we should be treated, the Soul knows that its body died and is not preoccupied with those thoughts whatsoever.

Wherever we go in life, whether in grief on the earthly plane, or for our life review in a different dimension, we always have a loved one nearby. This is not limited to a human form; it may be an animal, energy, or colour, but there is always an external strength to hold us, particularly when we cannot feel our own inner strength.

The Soul's Journey

Death is the biggest mystery on Earth from the human perspective. But for the soul, it is part of a larger journey, with each chapter holding a known expiry date. It's a human conditioning that transfers human experiences to the other side the Soul crosses through to be back to its original state in the most profound of transitions. The Soul understands the human ego and it understands our human emotions. If we are feeling guilty, they don't feel bad. They don't have the ability to do so. They understand that we are having a human moment and that we will soon understand our Soul's Purpose, once we reunite as one, on the other side. Death is understood, often celebrated, in this state of altered consciousness. It's always good to be back home.

The soul is a part of the Divine, and many believe that it knows the exact time and date when it will leave the physical body, regardless of how the earthly incarnation ends. In the section Life Between Life, we learned of how we have a known expiry date but are born with a sense of amnesia, so we cannot always recall our past life knowledge or our death date. Once a soul chooses to enter a body, such as the foetal stage of the life cycle, it will start to fulfil its specific life purpose, lessons and karma for this time on the Earth. Once fulfilled, the soul will leave and human life will end. It is thought that if one does not fulfil their specific lessons and purpose by the time death arrives, the soul still leaves the body, but will be born again with the lessons and purpose still to be fulfilled. This is what we know as karma, karmic debt, or the karma cycle. Karma is a collection of your previous choices, experiences and existences, that are believed to form the fate of your future existences, particularly in Buddhism and Hinduism.

As our very essence moves on from our physical vehicle, the deceased wants you to move on too. That soul wants you to feel the love and happiness they now feel on the spiritual plane, in heaven, or wherever you believe the soul has gone. Holding on to an attachment doesn't help either of you, and at the heart of the matter is love and letting go, but I know your human heart may not be able to perceive this in times of grief.

Reincarnation and Past Lives

Reincarnation is the rebirth of the old soul into a new body. Ancient texts told of compelling deaths and the wondrous and heroic journeys of the soul through the underworld, where they battled between good and bad, light and dark, and many other triumphed destinations. Every culture over every period in human history will hold certain beliefs pertaining to immortality and the soul, regardless of your religious or spiritual belief. We really are not that different, there is a sense of unity and oneness amongst us.

In my role as a past life regression therapist, I have regressed those who believe in an afterlife, and those who do not, but the results are the same. We are born into this world with a pre-obtained inner knowledge within our soul from our previous incarnations. As much as we can carry forward our well-honed abilities and skills from our past lives (think of the mere five-year-old Mozart who effortlessly composed a piano concerto whilst peers would barely be able to scale a small wall, or Joan of Arc leading an entire army during her teenage years rather than worrying about menstrual cycles and approval from the opposite sex), we equally carry fears and phobias (drowning, money issues, relationship problems), and a contract of how long we are going to stay on this earthly plane in this incarnation.

Whilst we will all experience physical death, we will all experience reincarnation again and again and again, repeatedly learning the lessons we signed up for. It is through this continuum that we always exist somewhere on some level of consciousness and how we will always be able to connect with our loved ones if we choose to do so. We can connect through our intuition, dreams, regression, psychic ability or mediumship, and other channels of resonance. Whilst death leaves us with a severe change of address, it is not such a severe shift in consciousness, and we are never truly alone. This brings us beautifully to the cross over from the difference between the Afterlife and the earthly Life Thereafter.

Life Thereafter

Life thereafter is for those of us that are left behind on the earthly plane of existence following the death of a loved one. After the initial death and all the unknowns that it brings, from the busyness of funerals, deciphering wills, sorting personal belongings, property and more, there will come a noted change of events. After this practical stage, life thereafter can be an eerie and silent place to be, and often a lonely time as you switch from autopilot to something partly resembling normality, whilst the initial well-wishers and do-gooders return to their own sense of normal life. We may try to run and hide from our own grief, and so it is only natural that others will attempt to run away from our grief too. At some point, we need to face our grief and our life of which we are running from, to live the life which we have left; it is just a matter of how we do this.

You may notice how family roles change, how the previous introverts become leaders, the stoic become vulnerable, and the parents need parenting. Grief can bring out the worst in you, but it can also unveil the best in you, as you adjust to a new life going forward that has been brought about from the old way ending.

The truth of the matter is that the only way to grieve is by going through the grieving process, and so we must allow ourselves the time and space to do so, which in turn can lead us to being open to more positive emotions too, such as joy, relief, and rebirth. There will come a stage in your life after loss where you realise that there are only so many words and well wishes of family, friends, and professionals that can try and heal you, but in truth, your grief journey, and your life, is yours and yours alone.

As we learned earlier, your grief journey may not be linear, more like a bowl of dropped spaghetti. You may hit rock bottom in those initial days, or you may carry on with your daily activities beautifully, only for the proverbial faecal matter to strike the fan months down the line. There is no set way forward, but there is a way forward.

Some stumble through the first year without the loved one, without any great awareness of self, let alone of life itself, whilst others go about the most cathartic four seasons of grief, as the consolidation of reality sees them having to live through each birthday, anniversary, and celebration without their loved one present. In the future there may be days, weeks, months, or even years, where the death of your loved one is not forefront in your mind, but as you watch a nostalgic advertisement, smell that certain aroma, hear a piece of music, you will be whipped back through the years, back to a shared memory. You may have a bad day at work and go to pick up the telephone to call them and have that stark reminder that they are no longer there. A one-off occasion that they are dead can overcome you like a whole season of grief in one day. You will make it through though, as whilst there is loss, there is love, and this is why your emotions are triggered. A tsunami of love and memories as a reminder of how much you mattered.

The world of grief is ever changing, just as your own personal world of grief changes. Whatever the emotions and timing that falls upon your grief path, here are some spiritual aspects to be mindful of.

Signs of a Loved One

Our loved ones who have passed over continue to play a part in our lives in many days and ways, including the delivery of our grief process that will lead to an important part of our personal growth. You are stronger than you realise and stronger than you feel. Without your grief reactions, you wouldn't have become more compassionate, loving, kind, resilient, independent, understanding, stronger, positive, or spiritual.

Your loved ones in spirit would love for you to know that you are never really alone, even though you may be feeling more alone than ever. When the weight of grief debilitates us – or leads us to struggles with our day-to-day routines due to our dwindling mental health – we create a dense and invisible barrier around us that our loved ones find difficult to penetrate in order to be heard or felt when only inches away from us. Whilst there is no longer a solid physical presence in our life, we can still sense the energy of our loved ones from simply sitting in peace and stillness. We can even feel them, talk to them, or even shout at them if we are still feeling angered that they left our life. On those days where you dare to unfurl, start to be open to the messages that are coming to tell you that you are not alone. These messages may come when you are fully awake, in the twilight state of dreaming and waking, or through those moments of deep sleep and dreaming.

Symbolic signs and messages can come from flora and fauna around us; butterflies symbolising a time of transformation, robins as a sign from spirit saying they are here during this new beginning, or bumblebees reminding you of your personal power and the need to seek out a sense of community. Flowers bring comfort too; dandelions tell us it is time to start healing from emotional pain, buttercups symbolise joy, daisies for new beginnings, and roses with their many colours, each holding their own unique message. When you see such symbolism in nature, research the meaning, and you will start to see that loved one sending you frequent messages, if you choose to peek out from behind your veil of grief.

You may start to become aware of feathers, with each colour holding different meanings, with white believed to be that an angel or loved one is nearby. Coins can be a message to remind you of your worth, shells associated with resurrection, and even a simple stone can serve as a message of endurance and stability.

As well as leaving objects, your loved ones can also move them too, and at first, you may think that your grief is driving you into madness as items appear to have been moved or missing. Quite often, despite numerous searches in the same place beforehand, they will be exactly back where you started, be it your keys, a book, a crystal, or paperwork. Sometimes, your loved ones will just tease you with a tweak, whether it is ruffling your curtains, scrunching up your freshly-made bed, denting your newly-plumped cushions, or adjusting or dropping items such as photographs, mirrors, and ornaments.

Everything is energy in life, whether it is the life force within you, money, or electricity, and loved ones with their newly-discovered and evolved energy tap into our earthly energies. You may experience TV interference or turning itself on or off, children's toys suddenly playing a tune, kitchen appliances starting up, or the flickering of lights, all particularly good fun for the departed. Telephones ring, be it landline or mobile, often at a time they would call or when you are feeling overwhelmed and really want to talk to them or hear their voice once again.

And then there is the wonderful cledon, one of my favourite phenomena, when your loved ones unknowingly deliver you a message through someone or something in passing. This can be hearing a snippet of a stranger's conversation or a song's lyrics playing on the radio which are just the words you need to hear. There is no such thing as coincidence, everything has a synchronicity. You are never alone, and as you start to become aware of the signs and messages around you, you may draw comfort from this new presentation of your loved ones, which may lead you down a more spiritual path than you ever envisaged for yourself.

The Grief Voice Box

Talking about death can seem so awkward and taboo, but when we think about it, the words we typically use to communicate around the topic of death are thrown around in our everyday expressions. We enthusiastically say we are "dying to know" and exhaustively tell how we are "dead on our feet" or even dramatically exclaim "I would not be seen dead wearing that" to a certain outfit. Each and every one of us brilliant souls is different; our personality, morals, life paths, and our vocabulary. Consequently, as a direct outcome of these variations, we will perceive, speak and act differently when we are communicating around life, illness, loss, dying, death, and grief.

I am passionate and driven to create a world where we can speak more openly about all of these lessons. Some of us will respond to life-changing situations with silence and avoidance, whilst others will courageously broach the griever and conversations, only to trip on our words or mutter some convoluted statement. Whether silent or stuttered, we tend to fear that someone may actually tell us their true feelings if we authentically ask how they are. How can we understand others' emotions when we do not always take the time or courage to look at our own?

Throughout my personal journey of fertility, I have been on the receiving end of all the classic go-to responses to loss, including "at least you already have a child", "things happen for a reason", "it obviously wasn't meant to be", and "I know exactly what you are going through". When family members died I would hear "at least she lived a long life" and "at least they died quickly and didn't suffer". What I have come to realise about all of these words and opinions is that I would rather someone broached me and the subject so I did not feel so alone or invisible in my grief. If in doubt, let the words out, as when you are saying the words, it means you are present for the griever, and actions can speak louder than our words. Let your presence be known, courageous one.

Communication at the end of life and the dying stages

Opening Up To Difficult Conversations

The adage "life's too short" is easily said but rarely understood until our time on earth is given a definitive – and sometimes shorter – timeframe. When a loved one receives a life-limiting diagnosis we become only too aware of just how precious life is, and we need to prioritise our time, meaning and purpose for the most conducive way.

People who have deteriorating health usually know what is happening to them long before a medical diagnosis confirms their suspicions, as they have lived each and every day in the body where the pathophysiology is occurring. Nevertheless, if the person believes that their family cannot cope with the news, it can be profoundly difficult for them to talk about what they know, experience, or need to say. This unease can lead to words being left unsaid, feeling alone, and uncertainty on how to broach subjects such as their dying wishes and final goodbye.

It is due to this sense of awkwardness that I encourage you to pay close attention to the dying as they may be subtly encouraging you to talk with their tester questions, assessing whether or not you are willing to engage in an emotive and authentic conversation with them. Questions I have witnessed tend to be around their health or belief systems, such as: "What do you understand about my health issues?", "Do you think I need to sort the house out?" or "Where do you think we go when we die?"

As time becomes more precious and poignant for the dying, they carry great fears and emotions within their tiring body, particularly fear of saying the wrong words, causing upset, being remembered in a negative light, their mortality, guilt or shame around past events, untold secrets, or unfinished business. There can be the occurrence of collusion, illusion or delusion, where they pretend everything's alright, which only consolidates their terminal agitation, rather than speaking their truth, and tying up loose ends, which can provide them with a sense of inner peace. What influences the ability to authentically speak is their personality (never been much of a talker, not trusting anyone with their wishes or story), trust and rapport with the listener or estranged relationships.

It is important that secrets, stories, memories, regrets, hopes and dreams can be aired by the dying, as a way of setting the storyteller free. Masks and inhibitions are often shed at the end of life, making way for a vulnerable beauty as the dying courageously lay themselves bare, often for the first time in their life. It is through the words of the dying that we can learn how to truly live our own authentic life, as we listen to what truly matters at the end of our days.

One of the fears frequently voiced by the dying is how their death will impact on those left behind. When you take the time and courage to initiate a conversation, this allows the dying to feel more at ease and almost gives them a sense of permission for them to share their words with you.

Encourage your loved ones to share their stories, thoughts and feelings, be brave enough to tell your views, so that you both reach a place of understanding whilst you are both still physically present. Final conversations are so important, for both the dying and those they leave behind. Endeavour to help them share their life lesson tales – the good, the bad, and the ugly – so that their memories and aspirations can live on long after they do, and so that you really get to know who they were as a whole being before they became a being labelled with their various roles, be it child, parent, or partner.

Communication is a two-way process, and so it may come as

reassurance to learn that what I observed – more often than not – is when we take the courageous step to share our own authentic story, it acts like a key to unlocking someone else's prison. When we share our truth, we can open a new understanding in the listener. If sharing your truth feels too much, do try and share a relevant conversation with the dying.

If you wish to avoid the words dying or death, you could ask about matters pertaining to their future health. You could ask, "If you become really unwell, would you like me to stay with you?" or "Have you ever thought about what you want to do with your paperwork?" If you do not like these kinds of open questions, you can choose short and simple statements of comfort, where no response is needed, like, "If you are feeling frightened about something, please do tell me." Either approach conveys that you understand they are not going to recover but you are available to talk about things now in an almost hypothetical sense. The dying may not respond at this time, but as we discussed in the chapter Dying, those who are dying become more tired with each passing day, so because they will not speak about it today, does not mean they will not speak about it tomorrow, or another day when you try again. Create the opportunity, as whilst it is not always easy to know how or when to talk about life, let alone dying and death, when time is so precious, today is a good time to start. Old photographs, letters and other memorabilia are a great way for breaking the ice and starting conversations. You can start creating new stories and memories with your loved ones so something of theirs will live on after they do, such as making a memory box, which is discussed more in depth in the next chapter, The Grief Toolbox.

I always encouraged family to talk and relive stories with loved ones who were unable to communicate, be it in intensive care units (ICU), post stroke, or in the end-of-life stages. It is thought that hearing is the last sense to cease in the dying body, so whilst you may feel self-conscious or unheard, I believe your words are still being received so let your words flow from you, as I cannot emphasise enough the therapeutic benefit this will have for you in the long term. I would encourage you to keep your communication simple and short, ask questions in a direct manner, and use gestures to enhance your words, particularly if there are hearing difficulties. Allow a gap where the loved one would have voiced the answer had they been able to, which they may be able to do in their mind, even though you cannot hear their response. You can fill the silent moments with looking at non-verbal responses, such as an eye twitch, a finger movement, or simply use the silence for your personal thoughts and reflection.

If your loved one is confused or does not recognise you, due to conditions such as dementia, you are still able to communicate. Be in a positive mindset and have a heartfelt intention to connect with them. Give them your full undivided attention, and position yourself so that you are in front of them, so that they can clearly see your face, mouth and hand movements. Speak in clear and short sentences, allow time for them to speak (regardless of whether or not they are able to do so), listen fully, with your ears, eyes and heart open. Do not be deterred by your attempts; depending on their tiredness, simply distract and redirect the question again. Research into dementia shows that whilst many struggle with speaking, music can access feelings, ideas, mood, and conversations, especially when we play a song that holds personal meaning to them. Whilst they may not communicate with you how you and your heart would wish, they can sing a song to show you they once lived and that they still hold joy within them. If they are physically able, you could hold your loved one and gently sway or dance, and communicate in this unique way.

Throughout this book I have used the term "loved one" but life is not always about love, and we have many estranged and unloved ones on our life path. In cases where family members are estranged, or where issues seem unchangeable, there may be no words, but I do think there is a real value in just presence alone, although each case is individual. This can be a difficult situation in the end of life where some family members will ban other estranged family members from visiting, despite the end of life being a time of closure needed for many, the dying, and those who will be left behind. If you get the chance to be alone with the dying, ask about their understanding of the estrangement and ask about their feelings for you. These questions are a privilege denied to many, due to family politics, or in cases where there is no time or opportunity. When time allows these bonding or bittersweet conversations, particularly where there is an estimated deadline, speak. If you are an estranged member and cannot achieve this through face-to-face conversation, try to communicate through other means, from communicating with healthcare staff to passing on messages, writing letters, or through meditation and connecting to the energy of the dying. Tell them what you wish to tell them; it is for the highest good of all involved.

Whether you are with a loved or unloved one, if you are still feeling overwhelmed in conversing with the dying, and your loved one is in a healthcare setting, such as a hospital, hospice or care home setting, talk with the staff who can offer you advice, support, or broach the subject and questions on your behalf.

Listening Well

It is not by chance that we have one mouth and two ears to remind us that we should listen twice as much as we talk. As well as having a heartfelt conversation, listening is one of the most important gifts you can share with anyone, not only in life, but also in dying. Listening is the most wonderful tool and opportunity if you fear of saying the wrong thing, or cannot utter any words or audible volume due to your emotionally-filled body and lump-filled throat. When we wholeheartedly listen, without judgement, expectation or the need to fill the silence, the deepest communication is still present.

When we are not using our words, we tend to feel a little braver and in control, so use the time to listen to focus on your body language rather than the spoken language. Maintain eye contact, lean forward towards them and their words, smile, nod, or place a gentle hand on your loved one. Our sense of touch is a simple human instinct and yet it can provide reassurance and comfort on so many levels. Keep your feet firmly on the floor so you feel grounded and stable in this emotive reality, undertake deep breathwork to calm both yourself and the dying, as they feel able to talk more freely to their receptive audience.

Just because time is limited and precious, do not feel that you have to talk all of the time. Your loved ones are tired, and your presence can often be as intimate and important as words, as they know they are not alone. Ninety-three per cent of our communication is non-verbal, so our silent language can speak a thousand words, and encourage a thousand words too. As always, communication is a two-way process, so look at the body language of the dying; does their body language match their words? Are they genuinely happy and relaxed, or are their hands clenched with anger, or are they being too jovial with their emotive story?

Whilst body language is of as much value as the spoken language, this does not mean you have to keep all your emotions in. If you have tears to cry, allow the tears to flow as much as your words and breath, as crying is a natural response to emotionally-charged experiences, so be true to yourself and your grief. The tears can provide a powerful release that can ease the days ahead, as you have released these pent-up emotions, which creates a space for feeling more prepared for the next few hours or days ahead. Authenticity is as key in life as it is in death, and openly displaying your emotions can also encourage the dying to release their own emotions, so grant them permission to grieve for the life and loved ones they are soon to be leaving behind.

Saying goodbye

The dying need holistic care, such as effective pain management which still enables them to speak coherently. Like an intricate jigsaw puzzle, these people achieve a balance between their physical, emotional, social, and spiritual aspects and wishes, they are surrounded by those important to them, and are in a place of acceptance or peace, which would constitute as being a good death.

Unfortunately, a good death is not always achieved in end-of-life care, and some people will not experience a complete picture of their life and wishes, more a puzzle that has been dropped or has pieces missing. I have witnessed people die without acceptance: young mums who will not be around for their children, elderly parents who do not want to cause pain to the children and grandchildren, an angry devout follower who feels let down by their God, former criminals who have yet to confess their past or seek forgiveness, or a person who is stuck in the denial stage of the diagnosis and clinging on to that last glimmer of hope. These people are a whole different level of wishes, needs, emotions, and communication requirements. At base level, they can be terrified, confused, anxious, upset, angry, or totally overwhelmed and unable to express what they're feeling. Your loved one may not be able to express to you exactly what is going on for them, as they may be finding it difficult to understand themselves, but if they are open to talking, try discussing other topics or notify healthcare staff, who may be able to assist your loved one with their emotions and thoughts.

When people are approaching the end of their life, there is a tendency to search for the meaning and purpose of their earthly existence and have an understanding of the afterlife, even for those who never had a religion or belief system in their life. Do not hesitate in reaching out to the healthcare, hospice, hospital, or care home staff, doulas, chaplains, ministers, priests, rabbis, and any other expert in spiritual care who can provide answers and comfort for the dying and yourself. You are never alone, ask for help and be open to accepting that help.

It is imperative that I say that whilst being with a dying loved one can be seen as a call of duty and non-negotiable, it is a highly emotive process and is not for each and every one of us. Not everyone is comfortable around those who are dying, nor do they want death to be the last memory, so always allow everyone to do what is right for them, their emotions, and unique circumstances. No "you were not there when they were dying" guilt trips or other skewed perspectives for many years to come. Promise?

Communication after loss and death

Say Something

Dying is not always considered part of living, and as a topic of discussion, it certainly is not one of our first topics of choice. When there is a loss or death around us or our friends and family, despite years of connection and conversation, we suddenly seem to falter and get all tongue-tied, or fall into episodes of silence. Just as in our everyday life, when we have moments where we can never seem to know the right thing to say, so continues the problem around loss and death. However, it is through my years of observations that I think it is more courageous and conducive to try and say something to the grieving, even if it is only a hello.

As awkward as you may feel as the onlooker, trust me, the griever is feeling as equally awkward with trying to make sense of their new-found reality, and they are struggling to find the thoughts, feelings and words for themselves, as well as for others. With one or both parties feeling discombobulated or hypersensitive around their choice of words, we can tend to shy away rather than step towards a greater and more unique connection, both during the dying and the grieving stages. However, it is when we avoid talking about what truly matters, or leave what needs to be said unsaid, that we develop additional emotions such as disassociation, loneliness, suffering, and distress.

It may seem tempting and far easier to avoid the griever altogether, but they probably need you more than ever before, even with your awkwardness. Keep their personality in mind, and focus on keeping your communication short and honest, like, "I wish I knew the right words to say," or "I do not know how you feel but I do know I am here for you." Just a simple "Hello" accompanied by a sincere smile can convey meaning to the griever, showing them that they are not invisible in their storm of grief; they still exist. Remember, you are not setting out to fix their grief or create a perfect speech, you are just being present as grief can be a lonely and scary place to reside on your own.

Some of us genuinely fear that our words will cause the griever to become even sadder, whilst others fear the tears may flow from the eyes of the griever, and they do not know how they could contain this situation should this happen. If you feel genuinely awkward about broaching the matter of loss, then avoid it in words by simply saying, "Please let me know if I can help you in any way." These tender words let the griever know that you are aware of their situation, and you are there if they need you. Simple yet effective.

Endeavour to display empathy not sympathy, as these are not the same thing and can make the griever feel very different. Empathy is our ability to understand and share the feelings of others, as if we were to place ourselves in their circumstances. Sympathy is a reaction to someone else's circumstances or misfortune. Imagine that empathy is like walking in someone else's shoes and getting a sense of how they feel, rather than sympathy which would be wearing someone else's shoes and feeling sad and overwhelmingly sorry that their feet hurt.

We all eat, drink, sleep and grieve in our own unique ways so saying "I know exactly how you feel" is never going to be a true story, even if you have both loved a mother. Your relationship with your mother throughout your lifetime would bring about its own experiences so that your grief would be different. Put your experience and feelings to one side and truly reflect what words would help you feel heard, supported or visible, and then bear this in mind for when speaking to others during times of loss.

Timing of Words

Timing of our words are an important factor for consideration. We can become complacent in life about the time we have, and often procrastinate about undertaking tasks, particularly so if we have a resistance to do so, such as talking about death. Whilst you may not feel it is appropriate to call someone the moment you find out about their loss, pushing the words forward to another day will only make the task feel even more overwhelming with each passing hour. Could you convey your words in another way aside from vocal? Send a text, a card, a voice message, or a gift? How would you like someone to treat you if you were experiencing a loss? Think of the griever and their likes and dislikes, and create your communication based upon this.

Grief can come with an ever-changing moment of emotion, so pin down how the person is doing at the point of your connection, by adding in the word "today". This small addition has a powerful effect on our communication. In times of loss and death, asking someone, "How are you?" – whilst it is better than saying nothing – can seem like a rhetorical question. Given the roller coaster of emotions we experience with loss, it is even more poignant if we break down today into sections of the day, such as "How are you this morning?" or "How are you this evening?" as the griever may well feel like they have lived through four seasons of grief over the day.

Death of an unloved one

Death can bring about different signs and symptoms when we lose a loved one, but the same can be said when we are faced with the death of an unloved one. Emotions when there is a death where no love is lost, such as an incestuous relative, abusive partner, the parent that abandoned you or an ex who you once loved many years ago, still surface. Remember, grief occurs when we lose something with which we had an emotional connection. All relationships are unique, and all grief is valid.

Whilst there may be some emotional expressions experienced with a loved one – particular words left unsaid, shock, confusion, and anger – with an unloved one there can be feelings of relief, justice, and closure. Whilst this may sound like a positive, it is grief nonetheless. When we lose someone who we already considered to be dead to us there can be such great questioning; what ifs, if only, and a great amount of questioning and analysis. You may have already spent days, weeks, months and years in your unloving circumstances imagining emotions and scenarios of how you will feel when they do die, and now the reality has occurred. You may not wish to stand by their grave and weep in death as they did not stand by you in your life... but then again you might.

If you are grieving the loss of an unloved one, all the grief signs and symptoms, and tools to recovery still apply. You have still experienced a loss and a death within your life, so be true to whatever comes up for you. If you are communicating and supporting someone who has lost someone with whom they had a difficult or estranged relationship, still use the same approach with words as you would when anyone dies; you are aware of the loss, how are you in this moment, and other supportive words and measures.

Whilst the relationship may have experienced or ended with difficulties, people come into our life for a reason, a season, or a lifetime. Everyone plays a part in the jigsaw of our overall picture of life. So, when this part is missing, we may feel incomplete for a while until all the other aspects of our life adjust and realign to fill the void.

The Grief Toolbox

In times of great challenges, we aim to survive. People will observe us from the outside looking in, and voice that they do not know how we do it, or question where we find the strength. If we allow ourselves to pause for a moment, we may just wonder the same – where is this gentle determination coming from? The fact of the matter is that we are stronger and more powerful than we realise, and certainly more so than you may be feeling in times of grief. Life is tough, but then so are we. Grief reminds me of the children's book, *We're Going on a Bear Hunt*, where we soon learn that we cannot go over it, we can't go around it, we have to go through it, until we come out on the other side of our story.

As we have learned throughout this book, the concept of grief has evolved, and in turn, so has its recovery process. In the past, such a great emphasis was placed solely on talking therapies. Whilst such therapies still provide a valuable resource to some, we all have different grief experiences and grieve differently, resulting in the fact that there is no one-size-fits-all solution.

Research by prominent psychiatrists, Terry Martin and Kenneth Doka, showed that whilst we all grieve differently, there are two key patterns of grief response: instrumental or intuitive. These very different styles of grieving existed on a spectrum, each representing opposite ends of a scale. Whilst there is an air of generalisation, instrumental grievers tend to be the masculine whereas intuitive grievers tend to be the feminine. However, there is a blended grief too, which combines both aspects of the grief responses – which I think is more realistic – given how much our experience of grief changes over time, compounded by the differences between individuals undergoing this great change, both inwardly and externally.

Instrumental grievers are the thinkers, rather than the feelers, so they may lack outwards expressions of emotion, be able to mentally separate from the loss, and prefer a quiet, inner reflection. However, not all is quiet with the instrumental grievers, as these grievers express themselves through physicality, and may be quite active as a result. Whilst they may not be able to emotionally fix the loss within their life, they will busy themselves with fixing things where practical solutions can be achieved, such as working on the home, garden, or their profession.

If you are supporting an instrumental griever, you will do well to use your logical mind to help them: breaking tasks down to manageable steps, creating distractions through chores, making to-do lists, creating a support network for them, using humour if they are more likely to laugh than cry, being an active listener, and providing a sense of respite from not talking about the big grey elephant in the room that is their grief.

As we know, intuitive grievers are the polar opposite, so they would have a larger propensity to undertake the conventional talking therapies. The intuitive grievers feel more than they may realise, and like to get a real sense of what is going on, both in the inner world of their emotions and the physical external world. If you are on hand for an intuitive griever be sure to bring a listening ear, open arms for hugs and holding, and plenty of tissues, as these grievers will be emotionally open and talk more easily about their sadness and pain, ask numerous questions, and truly believe that their words and feelings are "better out than in".

Due to our unique grief trigger, our gender, and our grief pattern tendency, The Grief Toolbox provides a vast resource of tools to help you with your own grief healing, and to help others on their journeys. However, please do not limit yourself to just the physical or the emotional tools, as it is imperative that we have a balance of masculine and feminine in our recovery, so that we are healing both the physical body as well as the emotional body and energies. Each tool and modality offers you its own unique healing to help you both with grief and through grief, whether it is to investigate your repressed emotions and thoughts, or to implement a daily practice of gentleness and movement.

Due to the plethora of modalities, and how overwhelming grief can be, I have simply listed each tool alphabetically, and with a brief overview for each, so that you can research and discover more for yourself about those that call out to you. So let us look at the A to Z of grief healing tools, as we endeavour to move you from A to B and beyond.

Acceptance

One of the difficulties around acceptance is that it can be unclear of what it is exactly that we are endeavouring to accept. Is it the loss itself? Our emotional pain? The new-found reality? Allow yourself time to sense what exactly it is that you need to accept in this moment.

Acceptance is the final stage of the five stages of grief postulated by Elisabeth Kübler-Ross, in which we accept the loss in our life and recognise its permanency. Acceptance does not mean that you forgive or forget, but rather accepting what has happened, without denial or excuses. Acceptance is not resignation, nor is it acceptance of the death, but moreover an understanding of the experience and the lessons within it.

As with any aspects of your unique grief, do not allow yourself to be pressured into accepting the loss sooner rather than later. Whilst acceptance may be quicker, such as in the case of long-term conditions where we witness deterioration, for many, acceptance can take years, and some may never fully embrace this stage. Acceptance is not even essential, as whilst you may not accept your new reality, you can certainly learn to live with it, even though the object of your grief is absent. Instead look at finding ways to grieve, heal, and connect to your true self as an individual, not as someone who has become defined by their connection with another. You are whole and not the other half of someone.

Do not become too focused on ticking the acceptance box, it is just one of many emotions that you may experience as life shifts forward. As each day passes, a new norm is created, and you may find it easier to accept a new way forward, rather than accepting the past event of loss. Realistically, we can never fully recreate a past relationship or experience, but we can certainly create new connections and memories which is a beautiful way of bringing a new purpose to our life. As we adjust to our new sense of self, and create changes, we are evolving, whether or not we are consciously aware of the transformation.

Acupressure

Acupressure is a needle-free alternative to acupuncture, which works by targeting pressure points within your body with a firm pressure applied through fingers and elbows. This application sends your body a signal to stimulate self-healing and regulatory mechanisms, which helps to trigger, disperse, and rebalance your life energy known as Qi (pronounced "chi").

Chinese medicine takes a holistic view of our body, and associates every organ with an emotion, and lungs are associated with grief and sadness. Our lungs are responsible for breathing in clean air and releasing the old, and it is due to this natural cycle that the lungs represent taking in new ways and releasing the old.

Acupressure practitioners are readily available but I am all for self-healing and empowerment, so you can undertake some self-acupressure practices yourself, which enables you to undertake the exercise as often as you like throughout your day and grief journey.

Interestingly, the Lung 1 (Lu 1) acupressure point is called "letting go" and is located below your collarbones, the first fleshy knot you feel as you move your hands downwards. These acupressure points (or acupoints) can be located by crossing your hands over like a resting Egyptian, and where your middle fingers rest are your Lu 1 points. You may wish to use the Egyptian way or you can swap your hands over to have a hand on each side of your body. You will be able to feel when you are in the right area as it may feel tender, or you may feel tearful as you touch the spot.

When you have located your Lu 1 on both your left and right sides of your chest, apply a firm pressure for two minutes, whilst undertaking deep and calm breaths.

As the two minutes draw to an end, inhale slowly and deeply as you gradually release your finger pressure. Raise both arms up and over your head like an early morning stretch, lift your chest upwards, and gently tilt your head back. Hold your breath for a few seconds, and as you exhale, allow your head to come back down and return your hands back to the Lu 1 position and apply your fingertip pressure to your acupoints once again. Aim to repeat this acupressure sequence five times for optimal benefit.

Acupuncture

Whilst similar in their application to acupressure, do not try acupuncture at home as this modality certainly requires a qualified practitioner. Just like acupressure, this Traditional Chinese Medicine works with the lung energy, as ancient Chinese texts stated that when grief was present, Qi, our life energy, disappears.

Acupuncture is the insertion of extremely fine needles through the skin at specific points on the body with the intention of manipulating blocked Qi. The aim of acupuncture in grief is not to push you through or instantly remove your grief in its entirety, but to aid your healing process in terms of quality of breath, releasing emotions, and to optimise your energetic functioning.

Affirmations

Affirmations are short and powerful sentences that are ideally repeated daily, with the aim of affecting both the conscious and subconscious mind to positively affect our thinking patterns, habits, mindset, and behaviour.

Our brilliant subconscious mind processes millions of pieces of information every second with our conscious mind having over sixty thousand thoughts a day, many of which may be far from positive. Our conscious mind is where all our logical and analytical thoughts are created, but that is just the tip of the iceberg, as the subconscious forms over ninety-five per cent of our conscious awareness, so is a vast reckoning force in matters of a positive mindset.

The subconscious mind may be outstanding in processing information, but it is not so brilliant at differentiating between the past and the future, so it is highly susceptible to programming a positive mindset and outcome for our future by using these daily positive prayers, ideally for at least thirty days. Try saying a positive affirmation as you wake and start each day, and as you relax and reflect at the end of each day, as well as whenever you feel your mind drifting off in a negative direction during your day. You may feel a little self-conscious talking both positively and loudly at first, but take a deep breath in and truly go for it, as you hold great potential and magic within you and your words.

Affirmations are powerful statements to flip your negative mindset to a positive, so I encourage you to try to create personal words that resonate with you and your journey. If you wish to start the daily practice now, try some of the following inspirational words:

I release all expectations of myself and others.
I truly love and accept myself completely.
I grow stronger each and every day.
My life is a celebration of their life.

Alexander Technique

The Alexander Technique is a psychophysical discipline that encourages you to become mindful of how you undertake your daily activities which in turn leads to you creating positive changes. Wearing comfortable clothing throughout, an Alexander Technique practitioner observes your physical movements, and then guides you through verbal instructions and hands-on approach, on how to move, sit, lie and stand in a more optimal way, for both your body and mind.

Angels and Spirit Guides

The term spirit guides tells of energies of a positive nature that connect and assist us when we need them most or can simply become a constant part of our everyday life.

Spirit guides are known as Angels, Guardian Angels, Archangels, Ascended Masters, Deities (Gods and Goddesses) and Animal Guides, all of which we look at in this toolbox. There are other spirit guides, known as Elemental Energies (Sylphs, Undines, Salamanders, and Gnomes). As guides are energy, you can also connect with earth energy including trees, flowers, elements, sun or moon. Where there is energy, there is the ability to tap into that power and communicate through thoughts, feelings, and other senses.

We are all gifted a guardian angel to protect, guide and support us, from our first earthly breath to our last. A guardian angel is exclusively yours, whereas Angels are available to everyone.

Angels are superior immortal beings believed to have been sent as messengers of God. They are often depicted as a human form with feathered wings, but this representation may be limited in its portrayal, as there are thousands of angels, whether they are from a different realm or here as an earth angel (angels in human body form who are sent to bring love and spirituality to humanity).

It is proffered angels are always by your side, and so we do not need to ask for their assistance, they will simply come into our life to provide comfort or protection during times of need. If you wish to call upon angels for support, this can be done through simply asking or setting a strong intention to connect. Many believe that angels are present at times of near death experiences and death itself, and you become aware of this angelic presence through a change in room temperature, atmosphere or lighting, rather than witnessing a fully materialised form. Do you ever get goose bumps or a shudder for no reason? This can be another sign that angels or loved ones are near. When a goose bump or shudder affects you, think about what you were doing when this happened. Were you asking a question at the time? Some people believe that when we feel a chill it is a positive sign and encouragement for your question.

Whilst you may not be able to sense or see the angels, you may be able to see what are known as angel signs, symbols or numbers. Whilst the following messages are often associated with angels, I believe it can also be our loved ones nearby and not purely an angelic presence.

Angel numbers are one of the most common phenomena, where you start to notice the same recurring numbers, such as the time being 11:11 or 17:17 or a car registration plate of 555. Angel numbers come to let you know that you are loved and everything is okay, but they can also hold more specific positive meanings and messages. Try deciphering the clues through your own intuition or by researching the Internet or an angel number book.

Angelic messages may come in an abstract form, such as cloud formation, coffee froth, bath bubbles, puddles, or tea leaves, and do not have to specifically look like an angel. You might find heart-shaped stones, coins on pavements, words with personal meaning recurring in a book or television advert, shimmering waves of light, or orbs of colour. Feathers, and particularly white feathers, have long been associated with the presence of an angel or loved ones. I love when a singular feather appears where you least expect it, but the feather does not have to come in its physical form to tell you that love and protection are nearby. You could see a feather in a magazine, on a social media post, clothing, or even as graffiti. When these messages pop up, try to connect the image with a question you've been struggling with or wondering about.

Angelic presence is not limited to our sense of sight, and so you may experience pressure in the ears, a ringing, or even hearing an angelic voice or celestial music. If, however, you have repeated ringing in your ears, it may be of benefit to consult your doctor, as it could be due to tinnitus, a condition that causes you to hear sounds that are not from an external source. When we are busy in our waking life, we do not always notice the signs or our enhanced senses, and it is during such times that angels or loved ones may bring us messages in our dreams.

Whether you are already aware of angels or wish to create a connection, one way you can do this is through creating an angel altar. It does not need to be a large display, a simple tray will suffice. There are no strict guidelines here, you only need to create a space that holds special meaning for you. Some people may love white and pink, but others may be more blue, green or purple. The idea behind the altar is that you are creating a space which feels sacred compared to the rest of your home, so when you are at the altar there is a greater awareness of your special time. As I say, go with what is right for you, but here are a few ideas of what to use for setting up your altar:

- A special cloth or tablecloth
- Candles
- Incense, sage stick or Palo Santo wood
- Tibetan cymbals (tingshas) or a singing bowl

- Crystals
- Pendulum made from crystals, wood, glass or metals
- An ornament or figurine
- Feathers
- Shells
- Stones
- Coins or other symbolic tokens
- Photographs of loved ones or sacred images
- Oracle or Tarot cards, either a deck or a card for the day
- Fresh cut or potted flowers or herbs

There is no right or wrong way only your way, so go with your needs and beliefs. As a suggestion, you can also try the following ideas:

- Play some relaxing music or a song that holds meaning for you.
- Light your candles and incense stick.
- Sit or stand quietly before your altar and take a deep breath in for three, and exhale for three, and repeat this pattern until you feel yourself physically relaxed. When in a relaxed and open state, allow your breathing to return to its normal pattern.
- Say an affirmation, intention or prayer of what you would like to achieve from this sacred altar time. It may be asking for a sign of their presence, or asking for assistance in your grief.

An affirmation could be along the lines of:

"Angels, please keep me safe today and always."
"Dear angel, I open myself up for healing."
"Please show me a sign that I am on the right path."

A prayer or intention tends to be longer in length, something like:

Dear Angels [you can name a specific angel if you want to connect to one in particular]. I am ready to embrace [insert what it is you wish to achieve, such as forgiveness or releasing your emotional pain] for my highest good now. Please help me to allow this into my life now, with ease and grace. Thank you.

You may or may not get any sensations or answers initially but even taking the steps to create some sacred time will have benefits. Aim to spend at least ten minutes a day at your altar as a simple but valuable daily practice. Thank your angels or loved ones for being with you, as even though you may not have been away, you are never truly alone. The more you practise these sacred moments, the more insight and realisations that will come for you. If you find the silence difficult, you can try playing a guided meditation through the Internet, YouTube, mobile apps, and DVDs. You can find meditations (whether angel or not) and the experience can be enhanced when undertaken in this space.

Animal Assisted Therapy

Animals vibrate at a higher energy frequency than humans so it is natural that they are so in tune with our emotional state. Animal assisted therapy (AAT), also known as pet therapy, is a guided interaction between trained handlers and an animal, whether they are a fish, guinea pig, horse, or other animal. The type of animal chosen depends on the therapeutic goals of a person's treatment plan but the most common form of animal assisted therapy is a dog. A grief therapy dog (also known as an emotional support dog, companion dog, or comfort dog) has been proven to be able to assist people in overcoming grief, which has led to a recent rise in the use of therapy dogs;

although interestingly, AAT has been around since the 1940s. Grief therapy dogs are now used in funeral homes, hospitals, nursing homes, schools, and hospices, and also provide support in situations such as funeral services, and counselling sessions.

AAT works well as there is an unspoken language between man and animal, which works particularly well for children and adults alike, who are experiencing physical or mental health difficulties. AAT increases verbal communication, social and empathic skills, lessens depression, improves self-esteem, and reduces loneliness, boredom and anxiety.

Animal Magic

Totem, power, and spirit animals are terms that tell us how we can utilise animal energy to help us through various life experiences with their guidance, lessons, protection, power, or wisdom. These animals can come to us through various forms, be it energetically, physically (such as a pet or familiar), dreams, meditation, or recurring images in our daily life.

Totem animals appear when we are experiencing challenges or uncertainty in our earthly incarnation. Each animal, from the tiniest ant to the largest elephant, holds a given meaning or symbolism, which in turn can shed light on your darkness. A totem animal's appearance may come to remind you of the need to adopt more of the animal's personality or specific strength.

Power animals are similar to totem animals but are thought to be gifted to you at birth, like a guardian angel. Whilst power animals will come and go during your life, they have also been known to act similarly to the synchronicity of the totem animal, and will come in for extra strength and guidance during times of notable struggles. Power animals can help us as individuals, but can also assist ancestors, our current family, communities, and beyond.

Whilst totem and power animal beliefs can be traced back through time, the sighting of our animal guides can be seen more readily within our new and digital age, be they a repeated sighting of a specific animal on packaging, magazines, advertisements, oracle card readings, social media posts, or a book cover.

Spirit animals are the spirit of an animal, like a pet that has died, and they are a spiritual energy rather than a physical presence. This energy comes to guide and protect you during a particular journey, whose characteristics you share or need to embody, just like the totem animal.

You may wish to discover an animal to work with for strength and insight, which can be achieved through finding a guided meditation, buying a cuddly toy as a light-hearted reminder of the attribute you need to embrace, or investing in some animal oracle cards so you can intuitively choose a card for each day or week ahead.

Aquatherapy

Warm water therapy is one of the oldest and most effective treatment options for people with physical disorders, but has benefits for mental health too. Aquatherapy is also known as hydrotherapy and aquatic therapy, and consists of structured exercises combined with the physical properties of water, providing relaxation, reduced physical stress and increasing our strength, power and endurance.

Aquatherapy is not for everyone, and there are many contraindications of use, including allergies to chlorine, cardiopulmonary disease, cardiovascular disease, common cold, contagious diseases, diabetes, epilepsy, fever, hepatitis, influenza, labyrinthitis, open wounds, recent surgery, skin conditions, tracheostomy, urinary or faecal incontinence, and urinary tract infections.

If aquatherapy is not suitable for you, you can use the healing power of water at home:

A Cleansing Shower

Whilst showering, envisage a cleansing white light, a rainbow of colours, or your favourite colour, cascading from the shower head with the water. As the water covers you, imagine the colours washing over you and cleansing you of negativity. Imagine negative emotions and situations going down the plughole and being transmuted back into positivity. This is a simple but effective method that you can practise whenever you shower, so you are regularly cleaning the body and mind.

A Relaxing Bath

Similarly to a cleansing shower, soak in the bath and see your troubles drifting away from your body, and allow them to be drained away at the end of your bath. To add relaxation to your bath, you may wish to use herbal salt sachets, Epsom or magnesium salt baths, if they are suitable for you.

A Nostalgic Paddle

When was the last time you went for a paddle? Was it in the sea, a paddling pool or a puddle? Life can get so complicated and we forget to find joy in the simple things, so allow yourself to embrace your inner child and go for a splash; be it playful bounce or an angry stomp, create some childlike joy. You do not even have to wait for the next rainy day, simply pour water outside and get nostalgic.

Archangels

Archangels are angels of the highest order and consciousness, who have been tasked with assisting us on our earthly journey. Each archangel has specific areas of expertise and can be called upon at any time for assistance, such as your grief.

Metatron and Sandalphon are unique amongst the archangels having both lived on earth as human beings prior to being transformed into angels by God, while other angels were only created to be archangels.

It is generally believed that unlike angels, archangels will not intervene in your life without your permission as they recognise your free will to create your own life path and choices. However, we all face times when we feel in need of an extra boost of angelic support, and it is during these moments that you can ask for help and they will come.

Asking through meditation, affirmations, prayers, and journaling can help you feel a connection with your angels and archangels. We can connect further with them by raising our vibrations through using crystals associated with each of them, although if you have a strong intention and have your own crystal preferences, please go with this.

Archangel Azrael

Archangel Azrael's name is often taken to mean the angel of death, and is known as "He who helps God" as he is believed to help us transit from death to the afterlife. Azrael is also Angel of Grief and helps comfort grief and the associated emotions, particularly letting go of anger or guilt, as well as helping you to sleep. He resonates with pale yellow colour, so if you are drawn to using crystals, try using yellow calcite or citrine.

Archangel Chamuel

An Angel of peace and comfort, who assists in resolving difficulties in communication, particularly arguments. Green fluorite, pink tourmaline and red jasper work well for connecting with Chamuel's energy.

Archangel Gabriel

Archangel Gabriel can also bring peace and comfort, working particularly well with children. If you are intuitive or enjoy writing down your feelings, Gabriel can help you with your healing and messages. Aquamarine, citrine, moonstone, and selenite are wonderful crystals to use when invoking Gabriel.

Archangel Michael

The sword-wielding archangel is a great protector, who can help shield you from stress and fear, assist with cord cutting (energetic connections to past events and people), accepting change and providing you with feelings of courage. Crystals linked with this archangel include amber, clear quartz, golden topaz and sugilite.

Archangel Raphael

Call on Archangel Raphael for health concerns, and physical and emotional healing. Work with aventurine, citrine, emerald, malachite, or yellow calcite. Please make sure you work with a polished tumblestone of malachite, as it can be poisonous in its raw form.

Archangel Uriel

Similar to Archangel Azrael, Archangel Uriel helps in the soul's transition to the afterlife. Archangel Uriel helps us with forgiveness, releasing negative emotions for a more positive future. Uriel can also help with wisdom, illumination and your inner strength. Uriel is often associated with haematite, obsidian, rutilated quartz and tiger's eye.

There are many guided meditations online or through meditation apps, which can be a gentle introduction to angels and archangels alike. Be open-minded to what guardians may present to you. I write these words as I undertake a meditation in the hopes of connecting to a well-known, celebrity status Archangel, but turns out my sidekick archangel is as down-to-earth as me and is the lesser known Archangel Muriel. Be open to the support that comes forward for you at this time, whether they come from the earthly plane or beyond.

Aromatherapy Massage

Aromatherapy is more than a pleasing aroma through items such as scented candles, room spray or perfume. It is the therapeutic application of diluted plant essential oils by qualified Aromatherapists. Modern aromatherapy has been around for about 150 years and is recognised for its physical and emotional benefits. Nowadays there is even clinical aromatherapy which is when specific oils are used for their chemical constituents which fight bacteria, virus, or fungus.

Aromatherapy works through the sense of smell and skin absorption, be it through products such as diffusers, aromatic spritzers, inhalers, steamers, bathing salts, hot and cold compresses, clay masks, and body oils, creams, or lotions for massage or topical application.

Through the therapeutic touch, toxins from our stress hormones can be broken down and moved along, whilst increasing the release of positive endorphins which provide us with a feel-good boost. In aromatherapy massage for grief, your massage can be tailored for your needs, depending if you wish to be nurtured or experience a more intense sports massage. You may want a full-body massage, a back and shoulders massage, or a simple hand and arm massage, as we are often left feeling lonely and without physical contact when we have lost our loved one. Massage without oils is still therapeutic and beneficial should you wish to experience this simpler form, and there are many types of massages available, with Swedish massage being the gentlest type of full-body massage through to a deep tissue or sports massage.

Whilst there are mobile aromatherapists that can attend your home, there are many available in salons and leisure clubs, so choose which one works best for you; in the comfort of your own home, or stepping away from your familiar environment.

Art Journaling

Art journaling is a book kept by an artist as a visual diary of their emotional health, thoughts and memories. Art journals combine every imaginable style, media and technique as a therapeutic and creative process to artistically express you and your inner world.

There are different ways in which to create the basic book itself, whether it is to buy a blank journal, an art pad with thick paper, or my personal preference, an old hardback book and blanking out its pages with white paint. Not only are old books free or cheap (maybe upcycling a loved one's hardback book), they provide an air of nostalgia, as well as secrecy, as they look like a normal book when stored on a shelf. An art journal can reveal your thoughts and emotions upon its pages, and it is not something that has to be shared with anyone, just like you would not share any diary of your deepest thoughts and secrets.

If you are using an old book, you will need to cover a page with white acrylic paint to form a blank page and leave to dry. You should also glue two pages together to form each page into thick pages which can take any art media you wish to use. This process of slathering on thick white paint to remove the words can be therapeutic in itself. In addition, if certain words stand out for you, you can leave these showing through.

You can use whatever materials you find, such as:

- Acrylic paints
- Watercolours
- Children's poster paint
- Pastels
- Felt pens
- Colouring pencils
- Wax crayons
- Paintbrushes (cheap children's ones will do)
- Gel pens

- Inks
- Nail polish
- Markers
- Old books, magazines, wallpaper, and newspapers
- Photographs
- Dried pressed flowers
- Feathers
- Scissors
- Glue
- Glitter
- Stickers
- Stencils
- Templates
- Hairdryer for speeding up drying process

Ensure you cover your working area with old newspapers or similar items that can be disposed of once you have finished. By protecting surfaces and surrounding areas, you can be as expressive as you need to be without your logical mind cutting in to worry about mess or damage.

Once you have your white background, either from using white acrylic paint or using a plain art pad, start the creative process. There is no wrong or right way, only your way. You may wish to tear up papers to make a background, paint, doodle, glue, sprinkle or write. You can share emotions, symbols, dreams and future plans. Many people like to write their heartfelt thoughts down on the pages, secretly conceal them with paint before adding an additional layer of entirely black wax crayon, then scratching sections or words away. Others do not use words, just different colours, textures, tools and pressure. Remember there is no right and wrong, and certainly no perfectionism, just unadulterated expression. After allowing the pages to fully dry, you may like to put a date on the page, before closing the book and filing away until next time.

Art Therapy

Art therapy is a form of psychotherapy which uses the creative process of art to both explore and communicate thoughts, feelings and emotions which may be too difficult or distressing to express through spoken words. Let me start by reassuring you that you do not need to be any good at drawing or art in order to try art therapy, as it is about the creative process rather than the final masterpiece. Art therapy encourages you to look at grief in bite-sized pieces and create a representation of the realisations that come up for you. Ensure that you have access to different art materials with a good range of colours and a large piece of plain paper. When you have as many tools as you feel you need, try this exercise for starters:

Imagine the piece of paper as being divided into two halves lengthways. You can fold the paper to mark the two sides if this works better for you.

On one side of the page of paper, left or right, express your grief as it feels right now, using colours, symbols, words, and anything inspirational that comes up for you.

In the remaining half, allow yourself to imagine what your life would look like once you have healed (either improved or healed entirely), and show this through colours, symbols, words, and other inspiration that comes to you.

With the two halves now drawn, connect the first half (the present) to the second half (the future). For example, this could be drawn as a bridge, path, or mode of transport.

Look at what you have created – is it a straight path or long and winding?

Is it a fast or slow mode of transport?

Are there any obstacles along the way?

Allow yourself to sit in silence for a while and note what realisations come up about your grief journey.

What surprised you?

What have you learned?

What would you like to change?

What do you need to change?

The final drawing need not be a certainty of your grief journey ahead, it is simply a valuable tool that encourages you to look at your grief in the present day, providing an awareness of your current mindset. You may wish to repeat this exercise every few weeks and date the drawing, or incorporate it in your art journaling, to diarise your grief journey.

Another simple art exercise is to draw a large rectangle or a large table, on which you draw all the things that you would like to share with your loved ones, be it past memories, your favourite food, or future hope.

If you are still feeling resistant to drawing, you can mindlessly doodle, throw paint on a blank canvas, or try your hand at colouring books, be it for an adult or child. All of these creative tools inevitably have a therapeutic benefit, so find one that works for you, and undertake it as often as possible.

If you wish to experience more intense levels of art therapy, research local or online resources to work with an art therapist who may be able to provide tailored activities for your grief.

Ascended Masters

Unlike most of the Archangels (with the exception Metatron and Sandalphon), Ascended Masters are believed to be spiritually enlightened beings that have once lived as ordinary humans within a physical body, as a means to acquiring wisdom and mastery required for them to ascend and become immortal.

You can call upon these great spiritual teachers, as well as angels, either for personal guidance or for your wider community and the world. Setting a strong intention to connect beforehand, you can work with an image of them, choose a colour or crystal that you associate with them, light a candle, read up about them, work with oracle cards, or undertake a guided meditation to meet them. If you are drawn to other forms of connection, communication, colours or crystals, please go with this, as you know what is right for you.

There are thought to be around sixty Ascended Masters, each with different interpretations of their attributes and colour, but for a brief beginner's guide, here are twelve of the most recognised masters:

El Morya

El Morya works with Archangel Michael and helps with power, confidence, strength, decluttering, Feng Shui, and shielding you from harsh people and situations.

Colour: Blue.

Hilarion

Works with Archangel Gabriel to help with healing, cleansing and truth.

Colours: Emerald green and orange.

Jesus

Jesus, the Messiah, shared messages of love, forgiveness, healing, unconditional love, and teaching.

Colours: White, green and yellow.

Krishna

The key figure in Hinduism, Krishna is about unwavering belief in the power of bliss. Despite many life challenges, he always managed to display happiness to all. He can help you embrace gratitude, positive affirmations, and with seeking out opportunities for growth and learning.

Colours: Black, white, yellow, and blue.

Lady Master Nada

Lady Master Nada or Lady Nada can be particularly useful in grief where there is conflict – particularly with females – in your life. She assists with forgiveness, power of speech, and is the unifier of families.

Colours: White, gold, lavender and yellow.

Lord Lanto

Lanto teaches the path of enlightenment and mastery, and helps with receiving wisdom and knowledge.

Colours: White and yellow.

Melchizedek

Melchizedek, believed to be an earlier incarnation of Jesus Christ, is connected with the Law of Attraction, esoteric knowledge, manifestation, healing, and change.

Colours: Blue, white, red, and purple.

Paul the Venetian

Paul offers the way of divine love through taking loving action in heartfelt deeds, and can help with creative expression.

Colours: Deep magenta and purples.

Quan Yin

Also known as the Goddess of Mercy, who embodies the divine feminine energy. She helps with love, compassion, letting go, unending sympathy, fertility, health, and forgiveness. Other spellings of Quan Yin include Kwan Yin, Guan Yin, Guan Yim, Kuan Yim, Kwan Im, or Kuan Yin, all of which are short form for Kuan-shi Yin, meaning observing the cries of the human world.

Colours: Red, pink and white.

Saint Germain

A master alchemist who assists with clarity, freedom, justice, opportunities, manifestation and all things magical. He can also bring inspiration to alchemy, education, healing, literature, philosophy, religion and science if these are your fields of interest.

Colours: Violet through to maroon.

Serapis Bey

Serapis helps with moving away from toxicity or situations that no longer serve you, be it a relationship, job, or location. He is a motivator for joy, hope and motivation, whether it is physically, spiritually or emotionally.

Colours: Gold and white, and often seen entwined.

Tara

A Buddhist goddess, also known as White Tara or Green Tara, who is all about purity, love, and our individual needs, be it about feelings, motivations, or being of service.

Colours: A rainbow of colours including white and green.

For any of these Ascended Masters, you can say a prayer of intention for what it is you wish to be assisted with. Allow yourself to feel calm and grounded down to earth, and at a time when you will not be disturbed for at least ten minutes. You may wish to have a pen and paper or journal nearby, to write any insight or sensations you experience. Feel free to create your own words of intention, based on your individual needs at this time.

As an example of a prayer, here is a basic format:

Dear Ascended Master [voice a specific name if you are drawn to one master for your particular needs], with love and gratitude in my heart, I ask that you help me [say whatever it is you are seeking guidance for]. Please step into my life now. In love and light, I thank you.

When your sacred time is over, regardless of whether or not you were aware of their presence, always give gratitude for their connection, and ask them to keep you safe and protected until you next reconnect. I like to envisage myself in a protective bubble, where I can clearly see my life around me but have a subtle shield to protect me from energies and opinions that are not for me to carry. Create a way in which you feel safer and more protected from outside influences, which may help you to feel a little braver throughout your waking hours.

Audiobooks

Audiobooks are a wonderful way to switch off, especially if you feel too tired to read for yourself. An audiobook can be one of your favourite books or genres, but if you specifically wanted a book around grief, you may wish to try one of the following titles:

- *A Body, Undone: Living On After Great Pain* by Christina Crosby
- *A Grief Observed* by C. S. Lewis
- *Finding Meaning: The Sixth Stage of Grief* by David Kessler
- *Good Grief: Heal Your Soul, Honor Your Loved Ones, and Learn to Live Again* by Theresa Caputo
- *Grief is the Thing with Feathers* by Max Porter
- *Grief Works: Stories of Life, Death, and Surviving* by Julia Samuel
- *It's OK That You're Not OK: Meeting Grief and Loss in a Culture That Doesn't Understand* by Megan Devine
- *Languages of Loss: A psychotherapist's journey through grief* by Sasha Bates
- *Men We Reaped: A Memoir* by Jesmyn Ward
- *The Long Goodbye: A Memoir* by Meghan O'Rourke
- *The Year of Magical Thinking* by Joan Didion
- *Wave* by Sonali Deraniyagala
- *We Are Okay* by Nina Lacour
- *When Breath Becomes Air* by Paul Kalanithi

Authentic Movement

Authentic Movement is about moving the body in an intuitive way which promotes self-exploration and improved mental health. Authentic Movement practitioners facilitate this therapy with individuals, couples, or group sessions.

Authentic Movement is believed to be particularly useful for those who struggle to express themselves verbally through traditional forms of talk therapies, as it encourages you to focus on your current emotional state and act them out through improvised movements, with the eyes closed, to heighten the body and mind connection. There is no choreography, music, or agenda, just free movement which continues until the mover feels ready to stop, with a maximum of thirty minutes of movement in any one session.

The process of Authentic Movement normally involves a mover (the person in therapy), and a witness (the therapist or other group members). Witnessing provides the mover with full and non-judgmental attention, something the mover may have lacked in life. The session concludes with the mover verbalising their experiences with the therapist, partner, or group, with the opportunity to receive empathetic feedback from the witnesses.

Authentic Movement offers participants an experiential way to work out their issues, and benefits include greater self-awareness, enhanced well-being and creativity, positive perceptions of the past, present, and future, and deeper insight and understanding of the body, mind and spirit connection.

Ayurvedic Medicine

Ayurvedic Medicine, or Ayurveda for short, is considered to be one of the world's oldest holistic healing systems and comes from a Sanskrit word meaning the "science of life". Deeply rooted in spiritual and philosophical traditions of India, Ayurveda is considered the art of living a balanced life of health, happiness, and longevity. Ayurveda is a vast topic, which would warrant a book in itself, but as a brief overview, let us look at the basics.

The ayurvedic belief around death is that it is the physical body that dies but not the soul. Those who practise Ayurveda maintain that each and every one of us is made of five basic elements: space, air, fire, water, and earth, which combine in our body to form three life forces, called doshas. These doshas each control a different body function, and whilst we inherit a unique mix of the three doshas, one dosha is usually stronger than the others. It is said that the health issues you develop are linked to the balance of your doshas.

The doshas are Vata dosha (space and air); Pitta dosha (fire and water); and Kapha dosha (water and earth).

Vata Dosha

This is considered to be the most powerful of the three doshas, controlling basic body functions, like cell division, your mind, breathing, blood flow, and heart function. The control can be disrupted through eating again too soon after a meal, fear, staying up too late or grief.

Pitta Dosha

Pitta dosha controls your digestion, metabolism, and appetite, and is disrupted by sour or spicy foods or spending too much time in the sun.

Kapha Dosha

Kapha controls body strength and stability, muscles, weight, and immunity, and can become imbalanced through sleeping during the day, and eating or drinking sweet, salty, or watery foods and drinks.

An Ayurvedic practitioner will be able to determine which dosha you predominantly are, and create a tailored treatment plan for you at this stage of your grief. The aim of ayurvedic treatment is to cleanse the body of undigested food, which may be achieved through dietary intake, massage, medical oils, herbs, and enemas or laxatives. As Ayurveda is a holistic healing system, it will contain more than these physical measures, and will look into all the senses in your grief and use cleansing therapies, colour, gemstones, meditation and sound to assist in the transformation of disrupted energy.

Bach Flower Remedies

In the 1930s, Dr Edward Bach left his lucrative Harley Street practice after years of being dissatisfied with the medical model of disease, whereby doctors focused on signs and symptoms, rather than the whole person. Bach went on to discover thirty-eight different flower extracts that he believed could be used to address emotional imbalances that were causing dis-ease within the body.

Agrimony	Self-acceptance
Aspen	Feeling safe
Beech	Tolerance and compassion
Centaury	Self-determination
Cerato	Trust
Cherry Plum	Calmness and rationality
Chestnut bud	Learning from experience
Chicory	Selflessness
Clematis	Being in the now
Crab Apple	Cleansing and self-acceptance
Elm	Coping
Gentian	Upliftment
Gorse	Hope
Heather	Empathy
Holly	Unconditional love
Honeysuckle	Letting go
Hornbeam	Easing exhaustion and tiredness

Impatiens	Encouraging patience
Larch	Self-confidence
Mimulus	Courage
Mustard	Brightness during despair
Oak	Strength
Olive	Easing tiredness and exhaustion
Pine	Positive self-value
Red Chestnut	Peace of mind
Rock Rose	Fearlessness
Rock Water	Easing shock
Scleranthus	Decision making
Star of Bethlehem	Transforming shock and grief
Sweet Chestnut	Despair and extreme depression
Vervain	Grounding
Vine	To soften the heart and thoughts
Walnut	Adapting to change
Water Violet	Calm detachment
White Chestnut	Removing unwanted thoughts
Wild Oat	Clarity of direction
Wild Rose	Embracing life
Willow	Forgiveness
Rescue Remedy	A blend for emergencies

Bach remedies are a solution of brandy and water with an extreme dilution of flower essence. The remedies are available mostly as a liquid in dropper bottles. You can either drop the remedy directly on your tongue or mix it into a glass or bottle of water to sip throughout the day. The dosage varies but most people tend to take several drops a few times a day. Some remedies are also found as capsules, chewing gum, sprays, skin creams, and bath salts.

Whilst Bach remedies are deemed safe and readily available to buy, do consult your local health practitioner before proceeding with new options in relation to your physical and emotional health.

Bibliotherapy

Bibliotherapy is used as a creative counselling tool, that uses reading books to positively affect our physiological and psychological well-being. Notable through reading fiction works, bibliotherapy can lead to three key elements: identification with the words, theme or characters, cathartic response to the text, and extracting insight from the text. Whilst a fictional book can help to positively impact on our mental health, I have witnessed great learning and healing from all types of texts, be they self-help books, spiritual magazines, online courses, old handwritten letters, a text message from a friend, or reference books.

Reading is one of many creative processes where we can only focus on what is in front of us in the present moment, providing us with snapshot sabbaticals from our everyday life. Reading provides a form of escapism, and whilst during times of overwhelm we may find ourselves rereading the same sentence over and over again, it is a process that we can easily recommence, which in turn provides us with pride and a sense of achievement.

Whether you wish to lose yourself in a fictitious story, learn a new skill through a reference book, read your favourite childhood book for nostalgia and inner child healing, or study one of these grieving tools in more depth, choose a text and commit to reading for thirty minutes a day. Working this into your bedtime routine can work particularly well as it allows you to take in and process more information as the mind calms, and can aid a better night of sleep. Whatever works for you will ultimately be beneficial, so find a time which is best suited to you and commit to it.

Bowen Technique

Bowen Technique, or Bowen Therapy, is a gentle therapy which is undertaken on a therapist's couch, or sometimes a chair, and uses fingers or thumbs to move over muscle, ligament, tendon and fascia in various parts of the body. This therapy is believed to trigger the body into resetting its own healing systems, rebalancing body energy, and achieving homeostasis; the optimal state of the human body.

Breathwork

We all breathe but often without a great sense of awareness until we are upset or stressed, and then we catch ourselves taking short, shallow, and erratic breaths. Consequently, this leads to us having less oxygen reaching our organs, and the body will not run as efficiently, so you may experience headaches, poor memory, or sleeping issues.

The good news is, through becoming more aware of our breath, and breathing deeper and more efficiently, we can turn things around and can actually reduce anxiety, stress and sleep issues, create a greater sense of self-control, improved posture, increased energy levels, and a boosted immune system.

As a starting point, make time today to simply sit and become aware of your breath.

Are you feeling relaxed or anxious?

Are you feeling tired or energised?

Are you breathing deeply or shallowly?

Take a minute or two to be present with your breath. Maybe you would like to breathe in the positive and breathe out the negative? Create your own words, which can be as simple as: "I am breathing in, I am breathing out," or "I am breathing in a healing light, I am now releasing limiting beliefs."

If you're interested in trying breathwork beyond these few moments, set up a relaxing space to aid your breathing further. You may even like to light a candle and play gentle music to blend out any background noises or distractions.

Beginner's Breathwork

Exercise One

1. Find a seat where you can sit upright and comfortable, with your legs uncrossed and feet flat on the floor, and with your hands resting on your lap.
2. You may wish to close your eyes, and then just allow yourself and your energy to gently settle, as you breathe normally.
3. When you feel ready to start focusing on your breath, inhale through your nostrils and hold for a count of four at the top of the breath.
4. Purse your lips, as if you were going to drink from a straw, and slowly exhale whilst envisaging all stress, tensions and negativity leaving your body.
5. You can even imagine breathing the negativity out into a Violet Flame, the candle flame or throwing into a campfire to be transmuted.
6. Repeat this pattern of breathing in through the nostrils, holding for four, and fully exhaling through the rounded mouth, until you feel notably relaxed.

Exercise Two

1. Find a comfortable seated position or lying down if this feels better for you.
2. Bring your awareness to your current breath pattern.
3. When you feel ready, place one hand on your lower abdomen and the other hand on your chest area.
4. Take in three deep diaphragmatic breaths whilst allowing your abdomen to inflate as you inhale and fall as you exhale.
5. On your next breath in, deeply inhale through your nose,

and exhale slowly through your mouth whilst making a long "sssssssss" sound.

6. Repeat this breath pattern for five complete cycles, before allowing yourself to return to your normal breath.

Alternate Nostril Breathing

Alternate nostril breathing is a yogic breath control practice, which is known as nadi shodhana pranayama in Sanskrit, meaning "subtle energy clearing breathing technique."

This breathwork can be done as part of a yoga or meditation practice, or as a stand-alone practice.

To practise alternate nostril breathing, try the following steps:

1. Sit in a comfortable position, either upright in a chair, or seated on the floor with legs crossed.
2. Rest your left hand on your left knee.
3. Using your right hand, exhale completely and then place your right thumb to close your right nostril up.
4. Inhale through your left nostril and then close the left nostril with your fingers, as you release the right nostril and exhale.
5. Inhale through the right nostril and then close this nostril and open the left nostril and exhale.
6. This completes one cycle of alternate nostril breathing.
7. You can now continue this cycle for up to five minutes, completing the practice with an exhale out of the left nostril.

Humming Bee Breathing

1. Sit upright and comfortably, allow your eyes to gently close.
2. Close over your ears with either your index or middle

fingers.

3. Gently rest your lips together and try to slightly open your teeth.
4. Breathe in deeply through your nose.
5. As you exhale, make a buzzing or humming sound.
6. Continue this breath pattern in through the nose and out through the mouth for as long as you feel able to (up to five minutes), ideally until you become aware of subtle vibrations throughout the body.

If you enjoyed this section on breathwork, you may also enjoy some additional exercises in the Mindfulness chapter.

If you experience light-headedness, dizziness or nausea during any of the breath exercises, please return to your normal breath pattern and allow yourself to remain lying or seated until the symptoms subside. Please use any of the breathwork with caution if you have pre-existing medical issues, such as asthma, or chest, lung or heart concerns.

If you wish to experience breathwork on a deeper therapeutic level, you may wish to look into Breathwork Therapy. Breathwork therapists, or Breathworkers as they are sometimes referred to, guide you through various therapeutic breathing techniques tailored to your needs.

Bucket List

In life after loss it can help to remember that our life goes on, even if it is in a way we never foresaw. Death makes us face our own mortality, and can inspire and encourage us to go on to live our best life whilst we are still able to do so, and drawing up a bucket list can help you with this.

The term "bucket list" comes from the saying "kick the bucket" which is slang for "to die"; coupled with the word list, it is basically creating a to-do list of things you wish to experience before you die.

This noted collection is all about your dreams, goals, hopes, and aspirations of what you wish to accomplish during your lifetime. Whilst you may feel uninspired to start creating positive changes in your own life right now, many grievers find it comforting and conducive to write a bucket list of what their loved ones wanted to achieve but were unable to in this lifetime, so that they can see their dreams through for them.

Whether you choose to create a bucket list of your wishes or your loved ones', the goal is to wholeheartedly commit to living your life. As I always advise, it is best to start small when creating positive changes, so that you do not become overwhelmed and give up. Simple daily achievements can be a daily walk, reading for half an hour each night, or starting to declutter the home one cupboard at a time. When you feel able to take bigger steps, and maybe even a leap of faith, you can commit to that marathon, write that book, study a new course, travel to that one place, or focus on the one key area of life you would like to change, be it physical, spiritual, emotional, or social.

For now, you could look backwards and start writing down all of your achievements to date, no matter how big or small. And then, when you have seen just how capable you are of manifesting greatness in your life, you can start compiling your bucket list of the road ahead. When you have compiled your list, turn your plans into physical steps of action, one positive step at a time.

Candles

Sometimes in life, or simply as the sun sets, we need to create our own light. By lighting a candle, we can invoke a sense of well-being. The soft illumination of a candle flame can help create a sense of calm and can bring us back into the moment with its presence. The flickering light and any accompanying scents can aid us in settling down into a meditative state. If you are a lover of candlelight, you may love the following tools: a simple candle meditation or the Tibetan Candle Ritual for grief.

A Simple Candle Meditation

A few moments before lighting the flame, create a corner of serenity in your home, grabbing any cushions or blankets you may wish to have with you for comfort. Turn off your phone and any other appliances or distractions as you give yourself permission to relax.

You can sit on a chair with feet flat on the floor or sit cross-legged on a cushion on the floor. Set the candle flame safely somewhere at eye level or lower, where you can look at the flame without slumping, and around a half a metre away from you so it is not too bright. Draw in a long, slow breath through your nose and as you exhale, say "let it go" as you release all the busyness of your day and mind away. Repeat this breathwork until you feel notably calmer and more relaxed. Try softly gazing at the candle before you, focusing purely on the flame. Your mind may wander at first, but just acknowledge your thoughts and thank them for coming, before bringing your attention back to the flame. Continue to gaze softly at the flame, gently blinking and refocusing your eyes when needed. If insight and messages come up, you can write them down once this meditation has ended, but just be in the present moment for now. When you feel you have completed this calming meditation, you can blow out the flame whilst making a wish.

Tibetan Candle Ritual

For those of you who have read the book, *The Tibetan Book of Living and Dying* by Sogyal Rinpoche, you may recall the beautiful ways in which the Tibetans view life and death. A gentle way in which Tibetans suggest releasing grief is through the calming use of candlelight, over a period of seven weeks.

You will need seven candles in total, one each of the following colours: red, orange, yellow, green, light blue, dark blue and purple. Each colour represents the colour associated with our body's basic chakras. If you only have access to one colour candle, you can simply imagine the colour of the week as you work through the Tibetan ritual. If chakras are something new to you, the next tool is about chakras, so you may wish to quickly browse through that section to enhance your understanding, and come back to this exercise thereafter.

Create a solitary and sacred time where you will be undisturbed from interruptions, maybe after a cleansing shower or bath at the end of a day.

On week one, select the red-coloured candle to represent the loss in your life.

Light the candle whilst sending out the intention to let go of your grief.

With a flame and candle position safely established, look into the flame whilst you begin to talk to the person for whom or the situation for which you are grieving. Allow all the words to come that were left unsaid at the time, the positive and the negative. Speak your absolute truth and release all the words and emotions within.

When you have finished talking, crying, expressing yourself, leave the candle to safely burn itself out. Write down any words or realisations that came up for you in a journal or grief diary, or you may wish to write them on a piece of loose paper so that you can then burn them in an outdoor space and bury them in the earth or throw them out to the universe to be transmuted back to positivity.

The following week, create the sacred time and space again but this time choosing an orange candle or imagining the colour orange, and repeat the same ritual. Try to undertake this weekly practice in the same place and time for seven weeks, working your way through the chakra colours in this order.

This seven-week ritual of letting go can be repeated after the initial cycle, for as necessary, until you feel ready to move forwards in your life. However, you may simply enjoy this weekly practice of expressing yourself and connecting with yourself and your chakras, which is therapeutic even if you feel unable to move on at this stage of your grief.

With any practices involving a naked flame, please do ensure the candles are placed in a safe and stable space, on a heatproof mat, and not left unattended.

Chakras

The word "chakra" comes from ancient Sanskrit meaning disks or wheels, and is believed to be a subtle energy system within each and every one of us. The chakra system is as natural as other systems, like our circulatory or lymphatic systems that process movement throughout our body to aid optimal health. Our chakras can become misaligned and blocked when we experience emotions such as grief or shock, consume alcohol or drugs, absorb negativity from others, or experience illness. When there are blocks or imbalances in the chakras, there will inevitably be a block or imbalance in our health and life.

There are seven main chakras, but it is thought there are actually 114 other chakras within us, and new chakras are being discovered over time, many which are external to our physical body. There are even cute mini chakras called "nadis" that further aid the energy flow within the body. The seven main chakras align with our spine, starting from the spine's base (root chakra) through to the top of the head (crown chakra).

Keeping the energy flowing freely within our chakras and body is much easier to maintain when we have an awareness of them. Each chakra is connected with different emotions and behaviours, colour, element, archetype (positive and negative traits), sense, shape, sound, life lesson, crystals and aromas (natural, incense or essential oils).

Root Chakra (Muladhara)
Our roots, physical survival, security, patience, and stability.
Colour: Red
Element: Earth
Archetype: The Mother or The Victim
Sense: Smell
Shape: Cube
Petals: 4
Sound: La or Lam
Life Lesson: Service
Crystals: Black onyx, black tourmaline, bloodstone, garnet, ruby, or smoky quartz
Aromas: Black pepper, clove, garlic, ginger, and patchouli

Sacral Chakra (Svadhisthana)
Creativity, abundance, warmth and pleasure.
Colour: Orange
Element: Water
Archetype: The Emperor and The Empress or The Martyr
Sense: Taste
Shape: Pyramid
Petals: 6
Sound: Ba
Life Lesson: Peace and Wisdom
Crystals: Agate, bloodstone, carnelian, coral, haematite, or red jasper
Aromas: Jasmine, patchouli, pine, and sandalwood

Solar Plexus (Manipura)
Willpower, self-worth, self-belief, decision-making and personality warmth.
Colour: Yellow
Element: Fire
Archetype: The Father and The Warrior or The Servant

Sense: Sight
Shape: Sphere or downwards triangle
Petals: 10
Sound: Ra or Ram
Life Lesson: Divine love and human love
Crystals: Amber, citrine, peridot, tiger's eye, or topaz
Aromas: Camomile, cinnamon, frankincense, ginger, juniper, lemongrass, musk, myrrh, rose, rosemary, and saffron

Heart Chakra (Anahata)
Balance, calm, serenity and love.
Colour: Green or pink
Element: Air
Archetype: The Fool and The Lover or The Actor and The Actress
Sense: Touch
Shape: Heart
Petals: 12
Sound: Ha or Yam
Life Lesson: Brotherhood, forgiveness, and Love
Crystals: Aventurine, diamond, emerald, green agate, green calcite, jade, malachite, or peridot
Aromas: Bergamot, frankincense, lavender, lilac, neroli, rose, rosemary, violet, and ylang ylang

Throat Chakra (Vishuddha)
Communication, responsibility, and purpose.
Colour: Blue
Element: Ether or Akasha
Archetype: The Communicator or The Silent Child
Sense: Hearing
Shape: Upside down pyramid pointing to the heart chakra or a Crescent
Petals: 16

Sound: Ga or Ham
Life Lesson: Divine Will and Speaking your truth
Crystals: Azurite, chalcedony, lapis lazuli, sodalite and
   turquoise
Aromas: Aniseed, camomile, frankincense, jasmine, lavender,
   neroli, rose, sandalwood, and ylang ylang

Brow or Third Eye Chakra (Ajna)
Intuition, clairvoyance, and clear visions.
Colour: Indigo
Element: Light or all elements combined
Archetype: The Wise Man and The Wise Woman or The
   Intellectual
Sense: Sight or Sixth Sense
Shape: Five-pointed Star
Petals: Two
Sound: Aum or Om
Life Lesson: Acquiring wisdom
Crystals: Amethyst, clear quartz, Herkimer diamond,
   labradorite, lapis lazuli, moldavite, moonstone, sodalite,
   and unakite
Aromas: Chamomile, frankincense and sandalwood

Crown Chakra (Sahasrara)
Connection, spirituality, and breaking negative patterns.
Colour: Purple, violet, or white
Element: No element
Archetype: The Guru or The Egoist
Sense: Sense of completion
Shape: Round skullcap
Petals: One thousand
Sound: Ah or contemplative silence
Life Lesson: Unity with the Universe
Crystals: Amethyst, ametrine, apatite, apophyllite, charoite,

clear quartz, fluorite, labradorite, Lemurian quartz, lepidolite, opalite, selenite, and seraphinite

Aromas: Frankincense, lime, neroli and vanilla calm

Cleansing and Healing

The chakras can be cleansed and healed in various ways such as sound healing, energy healing, or movement. You can self-cleanse and heal at home using these suggestions, or through meditation, affirmations, and adding colourful foods into your diet.

Chakra Meditation

This is a simple chakra meditation for beginners that is easy yet powerful. Follow the steps, and take around thirty seconds to facilitate healing each chakra in turn.

Find a calm and quiet place where you will not be distracted, sit for a few moments and allow yourself to settle down and set the intention to heal your seven chakras.

1. Start to focus on the area at the base of the spine, and start to picture a bright red light glowing and spinning motion in this chakra centre. Focus on this colour and movement as you breathe deeply in and out for around thirty seconds.

2. Next, move your focus up to the place just underneath your navel. Imagine a warm, orange glowing and spinning in time with your breath.

3. Move your attention up above your abdomen, and picture a bright shining yellow orb.

4. Focus on the centre of your chest and imagining a vivid green light or a soft pink light healing this entire space. You may wish to place a hand or both hands on this area and breathe deeply. Allow time in this area, taking as long as you need to heal this space.

5. When you are ready, move your attention up to your throat, and visualise a brilliant and powerful blue light moving in this area with each and every breath.
6. Next, bring your focus to the space between your eyebrows or your forehead, wherever you sense your chakra is. See a dark indigo blue healing energy spinning around in this space.
7. To finish your chakra cleanse, move your focus up to the top of your head and imagine a pure beam of purple light exiting your head and going way up into the cosmos above you.

When you feel you have worked through all of your chakras, imagine placing yourself in a protective cloak sealing in all the healing and positivity, or inside a thick bubble which can bounce off other people's energies.

Chakra Affirmations

Affirmations are short and powerful statements that are spoken in a present tense and repeated often to help formulate a positive mindset. You can use affirmations in all aspects of your life, including talking about your body and environment. Below are some examples of chakra affirmations, but you are encouraged to develop your own affirmations for the chakras you wish to work on, and what it is you are setting out to achieve. If you do not know where to start, remember that grief plays heaviest on our heart chakra, so this could be a good starting point for you.

Root Chakra
My root chakra shines and brings about positive change.
I am safe and secure.

Sacral Chakra
I am good enough and love myself unconditionally.

I am happy, healthy and abundant.

Solar Plexus Chakra

I am strong, courageous and decisive.

I express myself in an authentic and powerful way.

My solar plexus chakra and my life grow brighter each and
every day.

Heart Chakra

I truly love and accept myself.

I forgive myself and others.

I give myself permission to grieve and heal.

My life is a celebration of their life.

Throat Chakra

My throat chakra is clearing more each and every day.

I am safe to speak my truth.

I communicate my feelings with confidence and ease.

Brow or Third Eye Chakra

I trust myself and my intuition.

I am open to inspiration, inner guidance and wisdom.

Crown Chakra

I honour the Divine within me.

My life is moving forward with ease and grace.

Change Your Diet

It is always beneficial to eat a rainbow of coloured foods in
our diet, fruit and vegetables aplenty. If you adapt the habit of
combining a range of colour in your food choices (fruit salads,
smoothies and soups work well), you can balance all your
chakras every mealtime:

Root Chakra

All root vegetables (beetroot, carrots, garlic, onions, parsnips, potatoes, radishes, sweet potatoes, turnips), beans, cayenne pepper, chives, eggs, elderberry, nuts, paprika, peanut butter, peppers, pomegranates, raspberries, soy, strawberries, tofu, and tomatoes.

Sacral Chakra

All sweet fruits (apricots, coconut, mangos, melons, passion fruit, peaches, strawberries, oranges), carrots, cinnamon, honey, nuts, parsley, peppers, seeds, sesame seeds, sweet potatoes, and vanilla.

Solar Plexus Chakra

Bananas, brown rice, corn, fennel, ginger, herbal teas (chamomile, ginger or peppermint work particularly well), lemons, live yoghurt, millet, oats, pineapple, rye, spelt, squash, sunflower seeds, turmeric, yellow peppers.

Heart Chakra

All leafy green vegetables (broccoli, cabbage, cauliflower, celery, courgettes, kale, spinach), avocado, basil, coriander, cucumber, green apples, kiwi fruit, lemon balm, mint, peas, thyme, and green tea.

Throat Chakra

Apples, blackcurrants, blueberries, coconut water, fish, fruit juices, herbal teas, honey, lemon, pears, plums, sage, and water.

Third Eye Chakra

Aubergine, blackberries, blueberries, grape juice, grapes, poppy seeds, raspberries, and indigo vegetables.

Crown Chakra
Aubergine, blueberries, grapes, purple kale, red cabbage, rosemary, sage, thyme, and water.

Change Therapy
Grief itself brings about a plethora of individual change; eating habits, energy levels, personality traits and sleeping habits for starters, but loss is never a singular event and can create what feels like a never-ending domino effect. Whilst the thought of making a choice – whether small or potentially life changing – can seem overwhelming in grief, there are small changes you can start to create that may actually help with the grieving process and for making bigger changes in the future.

I am going to encourage you to undertake new activities to keep you occupied and to shape a new normal routine. It may feel like a huge contrast to life before loss when you would happily spend hours doing nothing in the presence of your loved one. However, this new-found void can be used for creating change, as whether or not you choose to actively participate in change, it will occur regardless.

Faith, belief and spirituality
You may experience a fundamental change in the fairness of life when a loved one dies, depending on your belief systems. We can either be strengthened and supported by them, or disillusioned and disappointed in them, as grief makes us look at our previously-held beliefs. When you no longer know what to believe in, believe in yourself. It is always beneficial to believe in something in life, but when you have those wavering moments, the only constant is you, so believe in yourself. You have a one hundred per cent survival rate through life so far, so start to believe in your strength and abilities, and you will have faith in life again.

Interests and Goals

Your previous interests may no longer be of interest, and even life may have lost its appeal right now. It is okay to let interests and hobbies fall to the wayside for the time being. Whilst you are in this state of change and disinterest, review your previous hobbies and pastimes to see if they were of genuine interest, or if they were merely habitual. As your life is already undergoing momentous change, you have a chance to start shaping a new way ahead. What have you always been interested in but never tried? See if you can find an online course, a book, or local class where you can start to make life interesting for you again. If you are wishing to bring more meaning to your loss and life itself, connect to something outside of yourself, such as volunteering at a hospice or hospital, start fundraising, or becoming a companion for your local community members.

I know it can be hard to look forward, but life will move forwards regardless of your level of participation, so I will always encourage you to actively engage in your unique life. Where do you see yourself heading? Do you have a goal? Set a goal that you would like to achieve, and start taking action towards it. Ensure that you are passionate about the goal and your end destination, so even if you zigzag along the way, you are enjoying the journey of new experiences, regardless of the outcome.

Priorities

What truly mattered in the past may have lost its poignancy in your life as it is now. You may have been a workaholic but now all that matters is your mental health, or connecting beyond yourself to friends, family, community, or a faith. It is so easy for thoughts and ideas to go out of your head, so consider making to-do lists, keeping a journal, writing things down on a calendar, or using notes around the house as prompts. Choose just one or two priorities for the day ahead, and let them become your focus. Small steps each and every day.

Routines

Grief is like a ninja that can sneak up on us when we least expect it but it can also be present every day as we go about our usual routine but with a key member missing. It is because of this daily reminder that we should be courageous enough to change the routine we have become accustomed to. This can be done in several ways, including rearranging room layouts, altering daily routine timings, changing your hairstyle or dress sense so that you do not look like the person you were, a dietary choice, taking a different route to work, or taking up a daily relaxation practice. Changing your old routine can help us with our mindset as it moves us on from living each day as an ongoing comparison to the past.

Relationships

Grief comes about from the many forms of death, and consequently grief can affect your relationships with yourself, friends, family, work colleagues, the community, or with the whole world. Some people grieve privately, others openly, but we all grieve. But with that said, so many are awkward around it and this in turn affects our relationships. Some partners and friends grow closer and more supportive, others will step away, possibly even run away. This is okay. In my previous book, I wrote about how people come into our life for a reason, a season, or a lifetime. If it is time for someone to leave your life, let them go. I know this is another loss at a time where you are already hurting from loss, but you need to be supported, not be the one to be supporting others, and certainly not chasing anyone for their connection.

During times of grief and life itself, relationships will come and go, but we are never truly alone. New people will step into your life with the most beautiful synchronicity, whether they are friends, family, healthcare support, community support, or a chance meeting. Be open to the connection, support, and new relationships ahead, including the relationship with yourself. You may need to get to know the new you, so embrace the relationship with yourself, as it is the one relationship that is with us throughout our life, from our first breath to our last. Take yourself out on a date. Pamper yourself. Drop the inner critic and speak to yourself with the kindest of hearts and words. Love yourself as you love others. You are worthy of being loved unconditionally. Today and always.

Responsibilities

There may be the need to juggle responsibilities in your life, whether it is in your home and work life, such as supporting the remaining parent who is now alone or organising childcare. Responsibilities, no matter how big or small, are best discussed aloud, so that everyone has any understanding of what is expected of them in their new roles. You could try drawing up a weekly planner, colour coordinating a calendar, or setting reminders on mobile phones. As with many changes, do not be afraid to ask for help, and equally, do not be scared to accept it. People like to have a purpose and be of use during uncertain times so start rallying up the troops.

Your life may be the total opposite of busy if your loss leaves you no longer being a full-time carer after years of this role defining your days and existence. In situations like this, use the free time for you, whether it is sleeping, journaling, decluttering, looking for a part-time job, writing a bucket list, or just being alone with your grief one day at a time. The change to the daily routine is already underway for you so start to fill the days with self-care where you tend to your own basic needs.

For the larger responsibilities and decisions, do take your time. Grief can cloud your judgement and we can be easily swayed during this time, so avoid committing to immediate decisions, allow time to be alone with your ideas, and write down pros and cons from your heart, not others' words. You can even make a list of tasks that need completing, and prioritise them in order of what needs to be dealt with first. Making one single decision at a time is less overwhelming, and with each choice made, changes will naturally occur, so when you make one decision, allow the dust to settle before moving on to the next decision.

Work and Finances

There are so many scenarios here, as maybe your loved one was the main breadwinner and you did not work at all, maybe you are the main breadwinner but feel unable to work. When we experience loss in life, be it health, confidence, or death itself, there is often an impact on our finances as we become unable to work due to many factors, be it emotional, social or physical. Start to look at what it is you truly wish to do for work, all those years you have had but never taken the leap of faith as you have been playing it safe. Brainstorm your skills and achievements from across the years, and see how these can be adapted and applied to your next job. If you are returning to work after a long time or for the first time, consider contacting a friend or your local job centre, or searching online for advice on how to complete a curriculum vitae, and interview techniques. If you do not need to work at this point in time consider undertaking some volunteering work which will not only break up your days, but will be a valuable addition to your curriculum vitae and work experience in the future. A job opportunity may even come from volunteering.

If you are worrying about money, ask for help. Whether it is asking friends and family for money or asking for legal or financial advice from a lawyer or financial advisor, ask for help during this time, especially if you are not used to handling legal or financial matters. These experts can help you in the now, as well as planning for your future.

Creating new dreams, learning new skills, developing new interests, shifting your priorities, and changing your routines, can bring positive changes to your life. Allow yourself to feel powerful and proud of the positive shifts for the future, as you start to live on, just as your loved one does in their own unique way too.

Cinema Therapy

Do you remember that one film that never failed to make you cry? This is why there is cinema therapy, as for years, films can provide such a powerful catalyst with their emotive content which can deeply move us and trigger repressed emotions within us, often in what seems an entirely unrelated story to that of our life and reality. Regardless of the film's genre, there will be many emotions, observations, and learning within, and often with a happy ending or sense of closure, something that you may be feeling is currently lacking in your own life right now.

You may find it helpful to have a notebook and pen nearby before you start the film (along with the obligatory snacks), so that you can journal down your thoughts, feelings and realisations, and be open to the mixed emotions and words that may tumble down on to the pages. Do not judge or strive for grammatical perfection, simply allow the conscious writing to flow along with your tears, be they of sadness or laughter.

Clairalience

Clairalience is referred to by several terms including clairolfaction and clairessence and means clear smelling. This is an unusual term but it simply means intuitive smelling. Just like our "normal" sense of smell and taste, clairalience is closely related to clairgustance (or clairgustience) which is our clear tasting.

Our sense of smell is the sense closely connected to our memories, as one sniff of a nostalgic smell can have us spiralling back through time to a specific memory or intense emotion, which is why aromatherapy and essential oils can be so healing in grief. When a smell comes at an unusual time, such as Grandma's apple pie or fried onions, a favourite flower, someone's perfume or cologne, cigarette or cigar smoke, we can take this as a sign that our loved ones are around.

As if this was not strange enough, you may be the only person who can smell it even though others may be present at the time, as not everyone can smell energy. We speak of such energy through phrases such as "I smell a rat" or "Something smells rotten here" as there is a strong connection between our intuition and sense of smell.

To develop your clairalience, smell everything! Do not turn your nose up to the opportunity of smelling the world after rainfall, flowers on a walk, fruit and vegetables in the supermarket, pets during cuddles, coffee in the morning, cooking smells in the evening, candles and incense. You can develop your senses further by looking at images in magazines, online, or on your mobile phone, whether it is a garden scene or a pizza advertisement, and bring the associated smell into your senses. When we strengthen our physical sense of smell we enhance other related intuitive senses.

In all cases of the clairs, please be mindful of what is coming through as genuine messages from your intuition and loved ones, and not grief signs and symptoms. If you are uncertain, please do contact your healthcare professional who can help clarify matters for you.

Clairaudience

Clairaudience – meaning clear hearing – is the ability to hear messages from the deceased be it through their voices, a piece of music, or other sounds. You may receive messages in one or more of these presentations, and there is no right or wrong, just our own past experiences and exposures working with us in this new intuitive sense. You may hear these messages in your own ears or telepathically.

When there is no physical source from which these sounds can come, like the peace at the end of the day, you may be more open to receiving messages. If this makes you feel uneasy, simply ask the noise to only come if of pure love, truth, and light, and for your highest good.

As with all clairs, the best way to enhance them is to develop a greater awareness of them, so for clairaudience, learn to be a more active listener. This can be achieved through paying greater attention to conversations with others, listening to song lyrics, listening to classical music and honing in on one particular instrument, undertaking guided meditations, and sitting in silence and listening to the sounds in the now (birdsong, distant conversations, cars driving by, or humming of electrical items).

Claircognizance

Claircognizance is a clear knowing that is unquestionable, it comes without emotion and simply is what it is. Unlike the other clairs, claircognizance tends to come when you're busy or undertaking a completely unrelated task. You could be having a shower, driving, cleaning the house, or gardening when this undeniable knowledge comes to you like a bolt of lightning, through words, images or thoughts. You will naturally question how you knew this or where it came from, but the sense of absolute certainty will not allow you to shake the clarity of your message.

To enhance your claircognizance, try guided meditations, journaling (first thing in the morning is particularly beneficial), or automatic writing (intuitively writing whilst in a relaxed or meditative state).

Clairgustance

Clairgustance (or clairgustience) is clear tasting, your intuitive sense of taste, which whilst it may not be as pleasant or as user-friendly as other clairs, it can still be of value and comfort.

As we already learned, clairgustance is closely related to clairalience (clear smelling), as when you smell a food you may also be able to taste it as a result of having already experienced it in your life in the past. The tastes can be your loved one's favourite food, or even the metallic taste of medicines and treatments they may have had at the end of their life, such as chemotherapy or blood transfusions.

If you wish to develop your clairgustance, you can start to eat more mindfully, paying greater attention to each mouthful. Is it hot or cold? Spicy or bland? Try varying your diet so that you are exploring more textures and layers of flavours.

Clairsentience

Clairsentience is our intuitive sense of clear feeling and is closely linked to our intuition. The feeling comes from an ability to pick up on the energetic vibrations of people (animate objects) and places and objects (inanimate). Some people have an awareness of a different energy to their own whilst others can intuitively interpret messages from the vibrations. Whilst clairsentience is all the same ability to sense and feel energy, when one feels the energy of objects (such as photographs or jewellery) and is able to convey messages, this is known as psychometry.

Clairsentience can often be felt in your gut area, hence why it is so closely connected to our intuition, our "gut instinct". However, in essence, it can be felt throughout our body (such as chest discomfort if your loved one passed with a heart or lung condition), pulling at clothes, touching of the hair or face, a tapping on the shoulder, or tingling sensations to name a few examples.

If you want to develop your clairsentient abilities, take time out to be alone in a place you will not be disturbed for ten minutes. Comfortably position yourself and start to slowly scan through your entire body from the top of your head to the tips of your toes, or from your toes up to your head. Repeat the full body scan until you start to intuitively sense answers coming up for you. What are you aware of? A colour? A sensation? Words? Be sure to journal down any insight that comes up for you. If you do not work well in silence, use a body scan or chakra guided meditation that can talk you through the steps.

Clairvoyance

Clairvoyance is arguably the most common of all the clairs, and means clear seeing or clear vision. Mediums are often referred to as clairvoyants, due to their enhanced ability to see things in the past, present, or future, which can be subjective, objective, or both. Subjective clairvoyance is using our own senses and experiences to interpret what is seen and why. The images are perceived within the mind, or the third eye chakra, which is associated with intuition. Objective clairvoyance occurs external to the body and mind, and is when we see spirit and messages before us with our physical eyes.

It is suggested that we were all able to see spirit as young children but lost this ability through our stories being dismissed as untruths by parents, siblings, peers, teachers, and the world. As it is merely repressed within us, it is just a case of tapping into our dormant clairvoyant skills.

Find a quiet time where you will be undisturbed to sit and focus all your attention on your third eye chakra, between your eyebrows, or your forehead area, wherever it feels right for you. Starting with the number one, visualise or sense the number in your third eye area. Does it have a colour? Is it 2D or 3D? Static or moving? Any other senses or messages? When you start to see or feel answers, and when you feel ready, move on to the number two. Continue working through the numbers one at a time, questioning and deepening their meaning each time. When you feel you have completed this exercise for your personal needs, say thank you to yourself and loved ones who were around you.

As you continue to work with this exercise over the forthcoming days and weeks, you can extend beyond numbers, to working through the alphabet (questioning if lowercase or uppercase, or colour, what the letter stands for etc). As you continue to ignite your intuitive spark, you can try symbols, everyday objects. What kind of font are they in? And then colours. Finally move on to visualising different items (such as common symbols).

If you wish to start with more guidance or feel uncomfortable in the silence, once again you can use guided meditations that encourage you with clairvoyance or third eye activation. If this feels a little too spooky for you, try a gentler theme of meeting a guide or angel, and go into the meditation with a clear and strong intention of receiving visual and spoken messages.

In all cases of the clairs, please be mindful of your messages. If you are uncertain about your newly-discovered visions or are experiencing other visual disturbances, please do contact your healthcare professional who can examine you to rule out any underlying physical health issues.

Cleansing Your Space

When our days and emotions are heavy, the negativity lingers around us. You know like when you turn up at a friend's house, and she flings open the front door with a dazzling smile, but as you step into the home you feel a tension in the air? The feeling of a "cut the atmosphere with a knife" situation, which reveals that the smile was covering up a recent argument. Everything is energy. It is important to regularly cleanse your space, and this process is often referred to as "smudging".

The ancient tradition of smudging is openly and regularly

used nowadays for cleansing your home and other spaces, after arguments, illness, endings, after visiting crowded places, for ambience, or to simply cleanse and reset your mind, body and spirit as a regular practice. Smudging is believed to work by the smoke's ability to attach itself to negative energy, which is then cleared, and transmuted into positive energy.

You can use a sage stick or Palo Santo wood to initially do a deep cleanse, and then maintain by burning incense. Palo Santo is a mystical tree that grows on the coastal areas of South America, and the name means "Holy wood" in Spanish. Palo Santo wood has been used for centuries for purification and cleansing, with many people believing it can help with healing, good fortune, spiritual protection, and restoring tranquillity, calm and clarity. Palo Santo wood tends to have a sweeter, more natural and earthy aroma to it, compared to a sage stick or incense, and personally I find it is easier to handle.

Your sage stick, or Palo Santo wood, can be lit at the furthest point away from your hand, allowing approximately twenty seconds for the end of the tip to be fully lit, and then gently blown out to extinguish the flame if the flame has not naturally extinguished. The tip should now be emitting smoke, which is what you require for cleansing spaces.

Cleansing Instructions

For a few moments before starting with the provided tools, find a quiet space to calm yourself and set a clear intention before you start the smudging process. Ensure to clarify what exactly it is that you wish to clear and achieve from the cleansing.

Light the furthest point of your sage stick or Palo Santo wood and allow it to burn for around twenty seconds before extinguishing with a gentle blow so that the flame is extinguished and only the cleansing smoke remains. Be mindful of any ashes that may drop and mark or discolour your surroundings or clothes. Please note that you may need to relight the sage or

Palo Santo as you go about your cleansing process, if smoke stops and cannot be encouraged back with gentle blowing.

Smudge yourself first, waving the smoke wisps a few inches away from your face, over heart and limbs, over the crown of the head and under the feet, if your mobility enables you to do so. If you have restricted mobility or balance issues, you can simply ask verbally or set positive intention to be fully cleansed, whilst standing with the smoke in your space.

Once you have cleansed yourself, you may start to walk around the spaces to be cleansed. Using your hand to waft the smoke into the furthest corners of the room, begin to walk around your space. If you have mobility or access difficulties, just send positive intentions or ask for an astral helper, such as a guide, angel, animal or loved one.

If you are cleansing an entire building, I would recommend starting in the furthest point away from the front door, on the highest floor, and methodically work your way from the top left side of the property to the right, and down each floor in turn. As well as moving from left to right of the property, and from top to bottom, it is recommended that you start on either the east of each room, or on the same side of the room each time, to ensure all walls are included and not forgotten.

Do listen to your intuition and sense of curiosity. If you are told to go about the cleanse in a different order, please listen to that, but ensure that all rooms are cleansed, as well as spaces between rooms, such as hallways, landings and walk-in cupboards.

Different sources will recommend different sequences, but I always start at the very top of the house and work my way down, before sweeping everything outside the front door (you can do this with a broom, intention, visualisation or voice – or not at all if it does not feel right for you). Likewise, many say to open all the windows before you commence the smudging process, but I like to keep them all closed during the process, and then open all the windows and doors after, as I feel that this fully condenses the smoke's ability to transmute the negative energy when the smoke is contained for longer. You will come to know what is right for your own sacred space; trust that intuition.

If you are prone to breathing or chest problems, such as asthma, then it may well be more suitable for you to open the windows prior to the cleansing process so that your area is well ventilated.

You can voice a traditional verse or prayer along with setting your initial positive intention or as you walk around smudging:

Shamanic Verse

Cleanse this space, remove the past
I've found my happiness at last.
Fill this space with Joy and love
Send Your Blessings from Above.

Cleansing Prayer

I am now choosing to cleanse myself and release any and all thought forms, beings, situations and energies that are no longer of service to my highest and greatest good. Across all planes of my existence, across all universes, and across all lifetimes. I ask that all energies that are less than love be transmuted for the highest good of all. And so it is.

Smudging Prayer

May your hands be cleansed, that they create beautiful things.

May your feet be cleansed, that they might take you where you most need to be.

May your heart be cleansed, that you might hear its messages clearly.

May your throat be cleansed, that you might speak rightly

when words are needed.

May your eyes be cleansed, that you might see the signs and wonders of this world.

May this person and space be washed clean by the smoke of these fragrant plants.

And may that same smoke carry our prayers, spiralling to heaven.

Once you are finished cleansing all of your space, it is a good idea to take any residual ashes of the burned herbs and return them to the earth, such as in the garden. Other endings are to add in sound, which can be as simple as going back through the property either playing loud music, clapping your hands, or any vibrational sounds such as banging instruments (cymbals, triangle, drum, although a saucepan and spoon works just as well) or a spiritual tool like a Tibetan singing bowl. It is recommended that you also either shower or take a cleansing bath after you have finished, to send the intention of washing away the old energy and encouraging fresh for a new start.

Cognitive Behaviour Therapy

Cognitive Behaviour Therapy (CBT) is one option for talking therapy which works by changing the way in which you think and behave. CBT is commonly used for anxiety, depression, insomnia, phobias, eating disorders, chronic fatigue syndrome (CFS), and is believed to be of value in grief. CBT makes us look at our thoughts, feelings, sensations and actions, to make us aware of how they are interconnected with becoming stuck within a situation or recurring cycle. With a new perspective of self observed and understood, our presenting problems are then viewed from a new vantage point and we can overcome situations and cycles through adapting new manageable steps.

You can access CBT by contacting your healthcare practitioner, who will be able to refer you to your nearest resource.

Colour Therapy

Colour therapy, also known as chromotherapy, is an ancient therapy which is about working with the healing vibrations of different colours. Each colour on the visible light spectrum has its own wavelength and frequency, which produces a specific energy in the form of colour which is believed to correspond with our emotional states. Light consists of the seven colour energies: red, orange, yellow, green, blue, indigo, and violet. Black is the absence of light and white is the full spectrum of light viewed at once.

Colour has been used therapeutically for thousands of years and can be added into your life through colour visualisations, meditations, crystal healing, plants and essences, home decor, attire and accessories, food and drink, or surrounding ourselves with colour (green grass, blue skies, or a black cinema).

Colour is absolutely intrinsic in our life and can hold different meanings in different situations, so let us look at the use and meanings of colour in grief.

Red

For passion, courage, willpower, endurance, action, energy, focus, confidence, and personal power. Red is needed to rebalance lack of enthusiasm, loss of interest in life, feeling insecure, feeling fearful or anxious.

Orange

Enthusiasm, fascination, happiness, creativity, determination, attraction, success, encouragement, and stimulation. Helpful in resolving stress, shock, inability to "let go", resentment, or a lack of interest in life.

Yellow

For enhancing creativity, concentration, and decision making, removing confusion, nervousness or exhaustion.

Green

A healing colour that helps restore equilibrium, and is very forgiving if you need to embrace change, let go, move on, and to nurture during times of personal growth and new beginnings.

Blue

In times of grief, many aspects of our life feel blue as we struggle to understand our loss. Blue is linked with expression and communication, and is conducive to help calm, relax, and reflect on our inner world.

Indigo

Indigo combines the blue of expression and communication, and red for passion and action, helping to express our truth whilst expanding beyond our current thoughts and mindset into a time of personal and spiritual growth.

Violet and Purple

Draw from it strength to forgive, find peace, contemplate, meditate, relieve physical, mental, and emotional pain, alleviate insomnia and restlessness, and provide a sense of stability when you are lacking balance in your life, body, or decision making.

Black

By way of definition, black is the absence of light which is comparable to death and grief. Wearing black attire during mourning has been strongly associated with loss and death for centuries, and was almost like a social status to show others you were grieving. However, black can also be used to self-heal in grief as it also represents power, strength, and authority, all of which may be required when undergoing change. Black is believed to be magical, protective, calming, stabilising, grounding, increase self-awareness, aid meditation, bring us back to current reality, and break down detrimental habits or routines that no longer serve us.

White

Whilst white is not a colour but a tone, it is still a powerful healer. White works well with healing negative self-image, harmony, Divine connection, simplicity, truth as it holds the energy and power of true transformation.

Community

We are often unprepared for the loneliness that grief brings. Loneliness can be a daily existence as we miss waking up with our loved one, shared meals, sharing conversations, and even sitting in each other's silent comfort. These feelings of loneliness can then lead to further detachment from others, as we struggle to be alone with ourselves yet are overwhelmed at the thought of being alone in a crowd. Loneliness can feel like another grief in itself, as it represents the loss of so many known and trusted ways of life.

Filling the empty space, that is loneliness, is a great challenge in our grief but one which we should try to fill with connection with others, and possibly in ways that we have never considered before. With our world now changed, we can start to create a new personal world through a sense of community, even though it may be an overwhelming step to take.

Community is a word used to describe a group of people living in the same area or sharing a particular characteristic, be it religion or grief. Community often provides a great source of solace, whether religious, spiritual, like-minded, creative or therapeutic in its service. A community can be a local, national, or international organisation, volunteering for a cause you are passionate about, voicing and listening to others, or paying to participate in an environment. Community can provide a kind word, a willing listener, a shared meal, and any number of large and small acts of assistance that help keep us afloat in the heaviness of our loneliness.

For now, just start considering venturing out by doing some research into your local area, to see what classes and groups are available. It could be a well-being group, an art class, a Death Cafe, or a pop-up event for you to try. Healthcare professionals now offer social prescribing, where they can refer you to community classes such as cookery, healthy eating, volunteering, exercise, gardening, arts activities and group learning, rather than the older tendency to prescribe medications.

Compassion

Compassion means "suffer with another" and is a deep feeling that arises when we witness another person struggling. It is more than an emotion; compassion is a strong desire to take action in alleviating the suffering you are witnessing.

In the initial moments of loss, when there is the practicality of responsibilities with funerals and property, there may well be an abundance of compassionate support around you. And, whilst many people will be there for the foreseeable future, people naturally gravitate back to their daily routines leaving you alone with yours. It is during this time of quieting that we need to learn the art of self-compassion; taking action to alleviate our own suffering.

When we begin to apply compassion to ourselves, we need to undertake an initial witnessing of our suffering, and act accordingly to help ourselves. I liken it to becoming your own doctor, becoming determined to get to the bottom of all your signs and symptoms, and with the gentlest and most loving of bedside manner, holistically heal the body and mind through small steps.

As your own healer, you can prescribe yourself treatments like taking time off, crying to self-soothe, eating nutritious foods, keeping a grief journal, undertaking gentle exercise, or learning one new skill per week. For other ideas of daily treatments, look through the sections on self-care and self-love for further inspiration.

Complicated Grief Therapy

Complicated Grief Therapy (CGT) is a psychotherapy which is used for depression and PTSD, but moreover complicated grief. This treatment can be undertaken as an individual or within a group, where you explore and process grief signs and symptoms, recreate imagined conversations with your loved one, improve coping skills, and redefine your life goals.

To assess whether CGT is suitable for you, do contact your healthcare or mental health practitioner, who you will be able to speak to about your current emotional health needs and provide you with a treatment plan.

Cord Cutting

Cord cutting is a spiritual healing process where one cuts energetical cords to release themselves from negative emotions, events and people. When we emotionally connect with others, we form an invisible energetic cord that holds us in the energy long after the situation or person has passed. Cord cutting is not necessarily about no longer loving that person any less, it is simply choosing to let go of any unhealthy attachments you have had. If anything, a positive connection can be improved because it is no longer exposed to negative energies.

If you are cord cutting with someone on the earthly plane, like an angry or manipulative family member, cord cutting can be used to take back your power and feel more detached from the negativity. Cord cutting will never mean the person disappears from your life unless you consciously choose to sever contact and not just sever cords. Cord cutting is more about taking all of your energy back into your own body, establishing healthy boundaries, lightening your sense of attachments or feeling pulled back in the past, be it emotionally, spiritually and energetically.

Cords can come in all shapes and sizes; we tend to see larger cord attachments to sexual partners, parents, children, siblings, close friends, and sexual abusers, with smaller cords noted with clients, teachers, bosses, co-workers, friends, and acquaintances.

You may choose to take a cleansing bath or shower before the cord cutting or you may feel more drawn to undertaking a bath or shower afterwards to wash away the negativity. Regardless of when you cleanse, do ensure you light incense prior, throughout, and after the cord cutting to help cleanse your environment as well as yourself.

To remove your cord attachments, you need to set a powerful intention for the following words to work. You can remove the cords however feels right for you, whether that is pulling them out like a plug, severing with Archangel Michael's sword and healing from the root upwards, pouring on a mystical elixir to dissolve the connection, working with a guide, colour or animal, or whatever visions or emotions come to you as the way in which to release you from this residual energy from the past. Trust it and go with it wholeheartedly.

Dear Spirit Guides/Mother Earth/Father Sky/Archangel Michael/insert your own guide choice. I call upon you now to help me release, destroy and transmute all energetic cords and connections that are not for my highest good. I ask that all cords from all lifetimes are now released, all cords are destroyed, all cords are now positively transmuted. All cords are now cleared, deleted, and erased from all lifetimes and never to return. All my unique energy now returns to me so that I am now complete once again. I ask now that I am filled with love, light, healing, vitality and protection, as I move forward. Sending love and light to those who are now released. Thank you.

You may need to repeat the mantra several times until you can feel a notable difference in your body or in your words.

If you wish to intensify the experience with visualising the cords being released, destroyed and transmuted, close your eyes in between the mantra. Cord cutting is personal to you and your past and future, so there is no right or wrong way to say or do it, just a strong intention of clearing and healing the cords, so do it your way with a heartfelt certainty.

After the cord cutting exercise, ensure incense is used to clear the area again, or fully cleanse with the saging ritual. As I said before, you may wish to take a cleansing bath or shower too, and then drink plenty of water to continue with cleansing your body, and allow time for peace and gentleness as the body readjusts to this lightness. You may need to repeat this cord cutting several times, particularly with the heaviness of grief, alcohol, or being around others' emotions.

Craniosacral Therapy

Craniosacral therapy is a very gentle "hands-on" healing where the therapist manipulates particular points around the head, pelvis, spine, knees and feet, to clear restrictions within the central nervous system.

This light touch therapy is believed to affect the pressure and circulation of cerebrospinal fluid around the brain and spinal cord, which relieves blockages and discomfort, and triggers the body's innate ability to restore natural balance and heal itself.

Crystals

Crystals are an established batch of molecules or atoms which may not sound very attractive by way of definition, but due to the many colours, shapes and sizes they come in, they are truly beautiful. If you are new to the world of crystals, you could purchase a tumblestone crystal or two to start with. Tumblestones are small, brightly polished pieces of rocks and minerals that you can carry in your pocket throughout the day. Each crystal, regardless of its shape or size, is believed to hold specific benefits for emotional states and life circumstances. Crystals that work exceptionally well with grief are as follows:

Amethyst

A powerful and universal healing and transforming purple stone, amethyst is great for instilling a sense of calm during times of stress, restlessness, anxiety, nervousness, as well as helping reduce insomnia and nightmares, and anger.

Apache Tear

A form of black obsidian, Apache tear has a gentle energy which naturally reciprocates your grief whilst transmuting negative vibrations into positive as you grieve.

Black Onyx

Black onyx is a fantastic stone for depression and life's challenges, as it can help with courage, vigour, grounding, and provide a sense of calmness, to help you keep stepping forward in life.

Clear Quartz

A colourless crystal that works well on its own for cleansing the body and mind, as well as being used with other crystals to help amplify their properties.

Lepidolite

A stone associated with transitions, lepidolite is composed of lithium, which is a medication used in mental health to help stabilise moods, making it particularly helpful in a grief journey when we may find ourselves susceptible to varying emotions. Even the crystal itself varies in appearance, and comes in pink, red or purple.

Mangano Calcite

This pale and creamy stone has an angelic vibration that helps with lifting you up, unconditional love, and healing emotional wounds.

Moonstone

This grounding crystal can be incredibly helpful when we are suffering a loss, as it is believed to ease feelings of shock and fear.

Pink Rhodonite

A calming crystal, pink rhodonite is pink with black veins, which provides the combination of unconditional love and grounding, so working well with grief, sadness, and denial, and helping relieve stress and anxiety.

Rose Quartz

Associated with love, this pale pink crystal aids forgiveness, healing, spiritual nourishment, and the ability to release denial and our truth.

Smoky Quartz

Smoky quartz is a healer, protector, grounder, releasing anger, fear, frustration and resentment, and beneficial in meditation, lifting mood, and bringing positivity back into our life.

Sugilite

For forgiveness, learning to live an authentic life, dissolving hostility, shock, trauma and disappointment.

New crystals should always be cleansed before you use them to remove any unwanted energies from them. You should also regularly cleanse your crystals to clear them of your own energies and those of anyone who has been around them. You can use any of the following methods:

Running them under cool running water and leaving them to dry in the sun or moonlight (the fuller the moon, the better).

Using lit incense, sage sticks or Palo Santo wood over them or nearby.

Sound healing with Tibetan cymbals or singing bowl.

Dance and Dance Movement Therapy

Dancing is largely understood to be light-hearted and fun, and whether we choose to dance like no one is watching, or dance because we don't care if someone is watching, dancing can boost our mood, confidence, body image, and provides an opportunity to have fun. While dancing is easily achieved and highly beneficial, Dance Movement Therapy (DMT) takes the therapeutic factors of dance to a new level, where dance becomes more than fun exercise – it becomes an unspoken language.

Dance Movement Psychotherapy (DMP), Dance Therapy, or Dance Movement Therapy (DMT), is one of the modalities of the creative arts therapies, which looks at the correlation between movement and emotion. DMP is said to work well with individuals, couples, families, or groups, and aids self-awareness, self-esteem, and expression of feelings. A typical DMP session will include an initial observation and assessment, warm-up exercises, supportive interventions, verbal processing, witnessing of body language and emotional expressions, and warm-down exercises with an emphasis on closure.

Death Cafes

The term Death Cafe can often trigger discomfort in many, as I discovered when I was setting up one in the UK. For clarification, I do not offer euthanasia over a latte, but I can offer you a latte at least, as hot drinks and biscuits are always readily available, along with a listening ear.

The Death Cafe movement was set up with the objective "to increase awareness of death with a view to helping people make the most of their (finite) lives" based on ideas by Bernard Crettaz, before being developed into The Death Cafe Model by Jon Underwood and his mother, Sue Barksy Reid.

Death Cafes are a pop-up event where people come together to openly discuss grief and death with no set agenda. The events are run by volunteers of the local community and on a non-profit basis, in an accessible, supportive and confidential space. I have over thirty years of healthcare experience and have witnessed how when someone's loved one's life ends, so does their own life to a certain degree as they become debilitated by grief, and struggle to see a new way forward. I knew this was happening in my local community, so with the mantra "participation not isolation", Good Grief – Northampton Death Cafe was born. We are not unique, there are Death Cafes in over 70 countries around the world.

Death Cafes enable you to speak your truth and share your story, whether your experience of death was three weeks ago or thirty years. Our grief journey has no specific timeline, but we can tend to feel sensitive or silenced when years have passed and yet we are still grieving, and so we stop sharing our story and memories. Death Cafes enable you to speak openly without judgement, with strangers, who often become friends.

You can find your local Death Cafe by visiting deathcafe. com, or searching on social media platforms like Facebook.

Decluttering and Sentimental Upcycling

The Swedish word "dostadning" is a hybrid of the words death and cleaning, and as harsh or morbid as it may sound, it is exactly that: the process of cleaning your house before you die, rather than leaving it to your loved ones to sort after you have died.

Death cleaning is not widely used, and so realistically, you may need to undertake the organising and decluttering of the deceased's worldly possessions until dostadning catches on. Decluttering is removing, organising, and prioritising mess or clutter, whether that is material possessions, your mind, or commitments. It is thought that a cluttered home leads to a cluttered mind, and when we start to declutter the physical, we begin to clear the mental and emotional.

Decluttering physical items after a death is different for everyone, some will not want to start clearing out belongings, others will lose themselves in the productive task and get rid of memories as soon as physically possible. You may wish to declutter on your own, whilst others may look for support, or need to be part of the family methodically working through things in accordance with the last will and testament of the deceased. There is no clear way I can tell you to declutter, but I will offer some ideas based on experience.

What to do with items can be overwhelming, so I tend to categorise them based on outcome: bin, donate, save, or sell. Bin is throwing away items that are of no use to others, such as dentures, or recycling bin for items like old spectacles, empty bottles, or packaging. Donating is something which is not of great sentimental value or use to you or the family, but could be of benefit to others, like clothing, household items, books, or CDs. Save can be something you save for yourself or save for others, such as a wedding dress, jewellery, old letters, and other sentimental items. Sell is for items that you are confident to sell and generate money from, be it antiques or other collectable items.

Whatever I get rid of, whether through binning, donating, or selling, I thank it for being part of my life, and send it on with love and gratitude. I do this for dead plants, clothes or household items, as they have all been around my energy and life, and do not want to end on a negative.

Another option for the items you are organising is to upcycle them thereby giving old items a new life, and this is known as Sentimental Upcycling. Sentimental Upcycling is almost endless in its possibilities, but here are a few ideas to inspire you: Clothing like shirts and dresses can be turned into aprons, bags, button jewellery, button art in a box frame, cushions, children's clothing, dolls clothes, fabric Christmas decorations, memory bear or animal, memory blanket or quilt, napkins or placemats, rag dolls, or snippets of fabric in a box frame. You can even unravel an old jumper and knit or create something new, like a dreamcatcher. Hats can be used for funky decorations or even converted into a lampshade or storage basket.

Furniture can be covered with decoupage or modern-coloured paints, especially chests of drawers, tables, and chairs. An old wooden ladder could be used as a book or plant stand, vintage suitcases can be used for storage, a side table or even changed into a chair or pet bed, and glass bottles into lamps or candlestick holders.

You can even have your loved one's ashes turned into unique jewellery so that they are always with you, and there are even some companies that turn the ashes into memorial fireworks, an artificial coral reef in the sea, a cremation tattoo where you have a tattoo created with ashes in the ink, or even pressed into a playable vinyl record.

Deities

A deity is a god or goddess who is considered to be divine or sacred. Similarly, to animals, angels, archangels and Ascended Masters, deities are powerful spirits whose energy and attributes we can work with during times of need or as a daily practice. As we have already learned through calling in other guides, a connection can be achieved through simply asking for assistance, having a clear intention, or creating a sacred space or altar.

There are thousands and thousands of deities, and like with other guides, each with their own strengths and purpose, but here are some that relate to death:

Hades
God of the Dead and King of the Underworld.

Kali
A strong Goddess associated with death but can also assist with matters of time, sexuality, and motherly love.

Lord Ganesha
Ganesha is revered as the remover of obstacles, God of beginnings, and can also be invoked to help with fortune, wisdom, knowledge, patience, purifying the soul, and for achieving a peaceful life.

Yama
Yama, also referred to as Yamaraja, is the Lord of Death, King of ancestors.

However, depending on your current needs and emotional state, you may wish to research for a deity that resonates more with you. Gods and goddesses are connected to the Sun, Moon, Sky, Earth, Hunt, Love and other qualities. Some of the better-known deities are:

Freya
Also known as Freyja, who is the Goddess of fertility, love, and sexual desire.

Hecate
Hecate is about crossroads, entrances, witchcraft and sorcery.

Isis
Seen as a Mother Earth figure, Isis is the goddess of law, healing, motherhood and fertility.

Ixchel
The goddess of the moon and the protector of pregnant women.

Thoth
God of wisdom and magic, who was believed to have invented writing and astronomy.

Whether you work with a deity, angel, archangel or Ascended Master, it is like any relationship in life in that it can take time to fully develop. You may be struck with beginner's luck, but in the main, there are no initial earth-shaking moments or spiritual enlightenment, but a deeper connection will form over time.

Daily practices may be a simple hello in the morning, a meditation, creating an altar, learning more about the deity (angel, archangel or Ascended Master), being open to their presence, a divination reading, putting out an offering, and ending the day with a prayer to them.

Drama Therapy
Drama therapy is the use of theatre techniques, such as drawing, stories, music, pictures, play, fairy tales and metaphors, to aid positive mental health and personal growth. Drama therapy is used in a wide variety of settings, including hospitals, schools, mental health provisions, prisons, and even businesses.

Whilst it is generally facilitated by a Dramatherapist, you can try this exercise at home for starters.

You will need some paper or your journal, and a pen or pencil, even paint or other art materials if you wish. Allow a time and place where you are comfortable, and will not be disturbed for around twenty minutes.

Start with setting the intention of accessing, finding and creating an image of your safe place.

In a position which is comfortable for you, close your eyes.

Allow your body and mind to soften and quieten as you bring your attention to your breath.

When you feel ready, move your awareness to your heart space. You may wish to place your hand or hands over your heart to intensify the focus.

Using your intention, say, "I give myself permission to connect with my grief."

When you take your next inhale, start to imagine your safe place to grieve.

When you have an image, words, or other insight, open your eyes and draw your safe place, adding any words or colour that came up.

Intuitively look at your drawing and allow yourself to imagine the picture talking to you about your safe place. What is it telling you? You may connect more easily if you place a hand back on your heart.

Write down what the drawing is telling you about your grief and your safe place. Do not over analyse, just go with whatever comes up, as it may be a metaphor or symbolism.

You can undertake this exercise whenever you wish to look into elements of your grief more deeply; it may not be about finding a safe place, but another question.

If you enjoyed this exercise but wish to work on a deeper and more supported level, look into working with a dramatherapist.

Dreams

As we discovered in chapter The In-Between States, it is all a matter of consciousness: our waking life, sleeping, dreaming, meditating, being alive or deceased. Dreams are a universal experience characterised by a state of consciousness where emotions, ideas, images, and sensations arise from the subconscious, and processes emotions, stimuli, memories, and information that's been absorbed throughout our waking hours.

Whilst we all dream, there are different types of dreams, including daydreams, healing dreams, lucid dreams, nightmares, recurring dreams, and prophetic dreams. Whilst many of our dreams are us simply processing the occurrences and emotions from the previous day or two, other dreams can provide mystical insight, and great reassurance and comfort.

As you drift off to sleep, set an intention to remember your dreams upon waking. You can also set an intention for the type of dream you would like to have, like connecting with loved ones during your dreams. Be open to how the communication comes forward in dreams, as it may be through telepathy, symbolism and metaphors rather than a direct and spoken language.

Similar to meditation, when our brainwave frequency lowers in sleep and dreaming, we are more open to connecting, both with ourselves, and with others, as the veil is thinned and the communication enhanced between the two worlds. You are as much spirit as your loved ones, just filling a physical body, so be open to your night-time connection being greater than your grief, and allow messages to come to you.

Keep a pen and paper by your bedside for impromptu note-taking of keywords, colours, characters, or messages of your waking dream recall. The dreamy insight you gain may not be presented to you in obvious words or imagery, more a bundle of symbolism and metaphors that will require decoding. But fear not, the messages and the dreams will recur over and over until you finally listen and understand the message being conveyed.

Emotional Freedom Technique

Emotional freedom technique (EFT), also referred to as tapping or psychological acupressure, is a form of counselling intervention that draws on various theories of alternative medicine including acupuncture and neuro-linguistic programming. EFT is used for anxiety, post-traumatic stress disorder (PTSD), depression, pain, negative beliefs and habits.

As with acupuncture and acupressure, EFT involves the body's energy meridian points, but is similar to mindfulness in the way it focuses on the present. You can work with an EFT practitioner or learn more about undertaking EFT yourself. If you are new to EFT, I would recommend watching online tutorials to observe the tapping points and techniques.

Before you start tapping, you need to look at your starting point in relation to the issue you wish to work on.

Identify Your Issue

Write down one issue or what you would like to improve, and rate the intensity from 0 to 10. 0 is for not a problem at all with 10 being chronic and affecting your life. This rating system allows you to assess the effectiveness of the tapping at the end of the session.

The Tapping Sequence

Before you start each round of tapping, create a simple sentence to repeat to yourself whilst you tap your karate chop point – the fleshy part of the outer hand. The simple sentence should acknowledge the issue and convey self-love and acceptance in spite of it. For example: "Even though I have [name the issue], I deeply and completely accept myself."

The tapping points then follow:

1. Directly in the centre of the top of the head.
2. The beginning of the brow, above and to the side of the

nose.

3. On the bone at the outside corner of the eye.

4. On the bone under the eye, approximately one inch below the pupil.

5. Under the nose, at the point between the nose and upper lip.

6. Chin, halfway between the underside of the lower lip and the bottom of the chin.

7. Beginning of the collarbone, where the breastbone, collarbone, and first rib intersect.

8. Under the arm, at the side of the body, approximately four inches below the armpit itself.

9. When doing the tapping sequence, use two or more fingertips, and tap approximately five times on each point.

If you are working with an EFT practitioner, they may tap your point for you, or they may sit opposite you and mirror the moves which make it easier.

Check Your Results

Become aware of your issue, and write down the new intensity on a scale of 0-10. You should notice improvement each time which would be noted through a lowering number of intensity. Continue to repeat the tapping sequence until the number has lowered and resolved to a 0 or has improved and plateaued at a lower number than the original.

There are no recommendations on how often you should do tapping, and it will vary greatly on the issue with which you are working. Some people practise three times a day, others weekly, and some only when an issue comes up.

If the process of EFT appeals to you, you may also wish to look into Meridian Psychotherapy, which is also known as Energy Psychotherapy, as it is a blend of psychological talking therapy with EFT.

Energy Bodies and Energy Healing

We are all aware of our physical body but less so about our subtle bodies; energy systems that are layers of vibrating energetic layers beyond our physical body. Along with the chakra system, the subtle bodies and subtle energy points create an inter-connected energy field around the physical body, commonly known as the aura or auric field.

The further you move away from your physical body layer into your auric field, the higher the vibration of the subtle body. The layers start with the physical body, and expand out to the etheric template, emotional body, mental body, astral body, etheric body, celestial body, and the causal body. Some texts quote other additional layers, but regardless of how many energy layers surround us, we do know that we are more than our physical body, be it energetically or consciously.

Energy healing restores the balance and flow of energy and works directly with the physical, emotional and spiritual energetic aspects of well-being. Our bodies have a great ability to heal and when the energies are balanced, these innate healing systems are fully functioning. However, during times of stress, our energy can be displaced and will need cleansing for our optimal health and healing potential.

You may have heard it referred to as energy medicine, energy therapy, vibrational medicine, psychic healing, spiritual medicine or spiritual healing. There are then a plethora of types of energy healing such as angel, divine, intuitive, pranic, Reiki, or spiritual healing. It is thought that the healing techniques are not limited to clearing the energy within the physical body, but within the energy bodies too, unlike other energy healing modalities we learned about earlier such as colour therapy, crystal healing, or Kinesiology, and reflexology which we will cover later.

Healing can be transformational when delivered with a powerful intention, so much so that you can even receive distant healing. As the name suggests, this is when healing is performed by a healer without the recipient being present. Healing energies can be transmitted over any distance. In addition, healing need not be limited to an individual, but can be lovingly sent to a family, situation, community, or even globally.

Equine-assisted Therapy

In the same vein as animal assisted therapy, we have equine-assisted therapy for processing our grief, as horses are without judgement. Due to their sensitive nature, inherent honesty, and beautiful intelligence, horses have the ability to make us look at ourselves, as they reflect back our current feelings, emotions, and intentions that we are presenting to the world.

Equine-assisted therapy (EAT) tends to involve a therapist and horse handler to work with you and the horse to help you discover more about yourself, create new ways of thinking, and to encourage you to reflect on your grief experience.

Therapeutic tools are carried out through specific exercises according to your individual needs. If you have never ridden a horse in your life, please do not let this discourage you from this unique therapy, as EAT does not normally involve any actual horse riding, and if you don't want to – you don't even have to touch the horse. The tailored exercises only require you to interact with the horse; you may be asked to lead the horse over a series of obstacles or to lead it in a certain direction, creating new thought processes, vocabulary and actions. After you have completed the exercises, the therapist will discuss their observations and allow you to share your own insights. If you continue with this form of therapy, you may come to form a connection with the horse, which can be incredibly powerful.

Essential and Sacred Oils

Essential oils are 100% plant extracts that are believed to play a key role in restoring our physical and emotional well-being when we use them during meditation or sleep, for a boost throughout the day, or in the home.

Science tells how our repressed emotions and trauma can come to be stored in our body cells as well as the amygdala gland in our limbic system, which controls our emotions, behaviour and long-term memory. However, this gland does not respond to sound, sight or touch, but through our sense of smell. This sense is the one that enables us to recall memories faster than any other sense when we smell something which we encountered in the past, be it a loved one's perfume, a certain flower, a chemical, food or drink.

There are over one hundred different oils each with their own unique aroma, uses and benefits, so go with whatever scent you are drawn to, and trust it is the one you need for you right now. As a general overview, the following essential oils are recognised for their use in grief:

Bergamot, Camomile, Cinnamon Bark, Clary Sage, Cypress, Frankincense, Geranium, Ginger, Kunzea, Lavender, Lemon, Linden Blossom, Marjoram, Melisa, Myrrh, Neroli, Orange, Patchouli, Rose, Rosemary, Sandalwood, Vetiver or Ylang Ylang.

I recommend using essential oils with a clear intention of allowing emotions to be released from your body, whether they are stored physically or emotionally. You can voice the intention in your mind or aloud, and choose the words that connect to your current mindset. Intentions could be along the lines of "I give myself permission to release any emotions that are no longer for my highest good" or "I now choose to release any feelings, be they past or present, of fear/abandonment/sadness" and as you finish your words, breathe the essential oil scent in. I would recommend undertaking this practice every day for at least thirty days, to see the true healing benefits.

Whatever stage of grief you currently find yourself in, essential and sacred oils are safe and effective tools to use when used correctly. There are contraindications in pregnancy, and for homes with pets so please do avoid if this is applicable to you or your home environment. In addition, certain oils come with caution such as cinnamon being an irritant, or citrus fruits causing photosensitivity to the skin making it more susceptible to light and sunburn.

The essential oils are best used in an electric fan diffuser or water-based atomiser, to avoid the inconveniences of dealing with water and fire, and you only need a drop or two of each essential oil for an effective aroma. Some people like to create a mixture of oils, but I would not use more than six drops in total for use. You may wish to make a combination of two or three different oils, which you could make with the two drops of each or three drops of the first, two of the second, and one of the third.

Aside from using around the home in diffusers and atomisers, you can use essential oils in a purposely-made necklace pendant diffuser, create a room spray or body mist, or apply to the body directly, although this application will require a carrier oil for dilution as it is not recommended to use neat on the body.

For a room spray or body mist, you will need an 8 oz small spray travel bottle, distilled water, and essential oils of your choice. As water and oils do not mix, some people recommend adding two teaspoons of vodka or witch hazel to the mix, but this is not essential, you can just gently shake the bottle before use. Fill ¾ of the bottle with the distilled water, and add ten to fifteen drops of essential oils. When spraying, avoid delicate fabrics on clothing or home accessories as the oils are liable to stain. Room sprays do work well if you are sharing space or have visitors coming, and need to clear the energies of negativity.

For essential oils to be used directly on the skin, you need a carrier oil which can simply be coconut, olive, extra virgin olive, jojoba, argan, avocado, sunflower, or grapeseed oil, but do be aware of any intolerances or allergies you may have when selecting your carrier oil. Although most carrier oils don't cause a reaction, you should always do a patch test prior to using.

To perform a patch test:

1. Add a small amount of carrier oil to the inside of your wrist or just below your ear.
2. Cover the oil with a bandage.
3. Monitor the area and check the area after 24 hours.
4. If irritation occurs, rinse thoroughly and do not attempt any further use on your skin.

Whilst there are experts in essential oils who may advise you differently, I would recommend you start by using a weak dilution of one drop of essential oils with one teaspoon (5 mls) of your carrier oil choice. Always store carrier oils in a cool, dark place, preferably in the refrigerator. You should ideally keep them in a dark glass bottle.

In addition to grieving, essential and sacred oils can be of benefit to those during the dying stage. The olfactory centres of the brain continue to function even when someone is unconscious, so they will be able to register the aroma in their subconscious, adding comfort and positive aspects to the dying process. Using essential oils can not only help with the physical, mental, emotional, and spiritual states for the dying, but also for their family who are in attendance.

In addition to the use of what we know as modern aromatherapy with its essential oils, there are also sacred oils. The difference between essential oils and sacred oils is that sacred oils come from an ancient tradition that can be traced as far back as Ancient Egypt when they were used by the priest and priestesses in combination with healing and dreamwork. These sacred oils were, and still are, used to treat ailments of the soul and spirit, to help the soul of the individual on a different level of consciousness. So, whilst many of the sacred oils may be the same essential oils as used in modern aromatherapy, they are used with a very different intention.

Modern aromatherapy is all about the smell, but many sacred oils are most unpleasant in smell, as they are more about the energy within the oil and how it evokes the energetic vibration in one's aura. Sacred oils are often used by soul midwives, who help the dying with their consciousness, healing, and transformation during their transition from their earthly incarnation to the Afterlife. Soul midwives are widely available nowadays in care homes, hospices, hospitals, and the home setting, and liaise with general practitioners and district nurses when a patient expresses wishes to die at home.

Exercise

Exercise may not have been a pastime in your life before loss, but any movement during grief is beneficial, as it releases neurotransmitters and endorphins, which help to boost and regulate our mood, and relieve aches and pains.

When we engage in exercise, it can help clear the mind, even if it is only for a few minutes, as we are focused purely on the exercise which can bring about a sense of calm and achievement. Once we undertake one form of exercise, the mind is more open to feeling motivated to try other new outlets.

I am not encouraging you to join a gym, as this would be hypocritical of me and my own levels of health, but there are many ways in which you can create movement in your day:

- Belly dancing
- Climbing the stairs

- Cycling
- Dancing around to a feel-good song
- Decluttering
- Gardening
- Housework
- Jogging
- Joining a local class
- Power walking
- Running
- Swimming
- Walking the dog
- Workout video
- Yoga

Feng Shui

Feng Shui can be dated back to over 1000 years ago, and is the Chinese art that believes our environment influences our health and well-being. Feng shui works with the elements, and grief is associated with the element of metal, which is associated with our lungs, large intestine, and our skin. When we work with the metal element and Feng Shui, the aim is to transmute our grief to nostalgia, as it is said that to get over grief is both futile and destructive to the soul. Nostalgia is the bitter-sweet feeling when we reminisce about the past but with the natural tendency to evoke the happy memories, rather than the sad or troublesome times which, in turn, helps us to heal.

According to Feng Shui, the metal element rules two areas of our life; one being creativity and children, with helpful people, and travel being the second. Energy (chi) can become stagnant when we hold on to items that no longer serve us, and in terms of metal elements and grief, the clutter and stagnancy would be found in children's bedrooms, and creative areas like art studios, playrooms, and home offices, as well as around children's items, art supplies, paperwork, and unpaid invoices.

Decluttering these areas and items can help create the transition from grief to a healthier nostalgia.

As we have already discussed earlier, it can be difficult to start decluttering or disposing of belongings, but you can prepare yourself for this process by allowing yourself a month or two of paying your respects first. Allow the first month or two following your loss to be everything it needs to authentically be, whether that is guttural sobbing or relief and joy. Choose a prominent place in the home, and create an altar where you can respectfully display a photograph of the lost love. You can add flowers, crystals, candles, their ashes, and other sentimental items in this sacred space, like you would create a meditation or angel altar.

When your loved ones visit or view from their new home, they will know they were loved, are loved, and that they mattered. You can undertake a daily prayer, blessing, meditation, or talking spot at the altar. Other Feng Shui practices for grief include crying, listening to sad songs, wearing white not black, hanging a metal chime outside your front door, adding spices to your food (chilli, curry or ginger work well), going for a walk or meditating at sunset.

When this time has passed, be it one month or two, give thanks to the sacred space as you dismantle the altar. You can keep the photograph in a memory box or journal, or you can choose to continue to display it in your home, but acknowledge the end of the altar. Ashes can be returned to the elements of earth or water (if this is in accordance with the deceased's wishes) or kept in your home. If you choose to keep the ashes out of sight in a cupboard, it is deemed more respectful to keep them at heart level height.

With the altar dismantled, and the other practices considered, it is time to begin the decluttering process, starting with your creative and children's space, and facing that pile of paperwork. Thank everything that has come into your life as it, and you move on to the next stage of life.

Foot Reading

We have all heard of palm reading, but what about foot reading? Our feet are often neglected and we take them for granted, but they may just hold messages yet to be revealed to us. There are a few foot reading practitioners around but you can try interpreting your own foot reading too.

First, you can look at the colour of the soles of your feet, as colour is thought to indicate the following emotions:

- Blue: feeling hurt
- Red: anger
- White: exhausted
- Yellow: feeling fed up

Grief is very much an emotional journey which causes many physical imbalances and presentations, which in foot reading are believed to appear in the following signs:

- Athlete's Foot is a sign that someone is getting on your nerves and preventing you from moving forward
- Blisters can mean someone is rubbing you up the wrong way
- Bunions mean you do more for others than you do for yourself
- Corns can be a sign of protecting a personal issue
- Calluses (hard skin) may also represent an area of protection, such as repressed emotions or feeling extremely vulnerable
- Cracked heels suggest obstacles you must overcome before you can move forward, or feel divided and torn
- Damp skin could be a sign of too much toxicity or anxiety
- Deep crevices can be feeling divided or overwhelmed

- Dry skin is the need for more love and comfort in your life
- Flat feet indicate a very sociable person who accepts support from others
- High arches show an independent person who struggles to accept help
- Itchy skin quite literally means feeling irritated
- Oedema (swelling) in the reflexes is an emotion that has been building up over time
- Prominent capillaries and veins can tell of subconscious and deep-rooted hurt
- Peeling is a little like a snake shedding their skin; a fresh new start
- Rough skin may mean you have been or are going through a rough time
- Rubbery-feeling skin can be a lack of vitality and times of uncertainty
- Scars are past pains that are being concealed
- Temporary marks are fleeting emotions, thoughts and ideas
- Thick skin literally means thick skinned, strong willed and often insensitive
- Verrucas are usually a sign of a deep-rooted issue
- Wounds are old injuries leaving their mark or resurfacing
- Wrinkled skin can be feeling drained or troubled.

By researching a reflexology foot illustration online we can note how different areas of the feet are associated with different areas of the body. So, if you had calluses (hard skin) on the neck of your big toe (which represents the throat), this would translate as repressed emotions around communication. In addition to the emotion and the affected body part, take note if the condition is on your left foot or your right, as the right foot relates to our past, whereas the left foot is what we are currently experiencing in the present.

If you enjoyed working with your feet, you may be drawn into researching into Reflexology, which is where a practitioner applies pressure-point therapy to certain points and reflex zones on your feet, to help treat problems within your body-mind system.

If you are experiencing any foot conditions particularly Athlete's Foot, itchy skin, oedema, and verrucas, please consult your local pharmacist or healthcare professional for a check-up as you may require a treatment.

Forgiveness

Psychologists define forgiveness as a conscious, deliberate decision to release feelings of resentment or vengeance toward a person or group who has harmed you, regardless of whether they actually deserve your forgiveness. Forgiveness does not mean forgetting, nor does it mean condoning or excusing offenses that have happened to or around you. Forgiveness is not even about the other person, it is about you. Negative thoughts of resentment, anger, and hatred occupy space in your head and life, so whilst it may feel impossible right now, listen to some of my suggestions on how to release negativity, and create space and peace in your sacred life.

When we struggle to forgive, it is often because we are assigning greater importance to the past rather than the present or our future. When our thoughts, words, and dreams are lamenting the olden days, you will not see the beauty, potential, lessons, or happiness in the present day. "I remember when..." or "If only I had..." are all negative ways in which you are choosing to be with the past.

In cases of abuse, abandonment, and suicide, many questions or apologies remain unanswered, leaving us feeling unable to move on. No one expects you to fully declare love of the person or the past situation, but I believe you owe it to yourself and your life to try sending a sense of healing or love to the situation in some way.

- Writing an authentic letter or eulogy to the perpetrator
- Write a letter to your younger self from your older and wiser self
- Give yourself permission to release the past
- Acknowledge and voice aloud your understanding of the past situation or person
- Accept that there are no mistakes only life experience
- Seek clarity of what you want and don't want in your future based on past lessons learned
- Meditations on forgiveness, whether it is forgiveness to a person or situation, or self-forgiveness

Ho'oponopono – This is a Hawaiian mantra that was used by the Kahuna, the mystic healers. This simple practice is undertaken by closing your eyes and envisaging the person or situation that needs forgiveness or reconciliation. With a heartfelt intention to heal, repeat the words:

"I am sorry, please forgive me, I love you, thank you."

Forgiveness is such a vast topic, but I truly hope some of these words will resonate with you, and inspire you to start forgiving the past, others, and yourself for past chapters so that you can write more positive chapters in your life story.

Future Life Progression

Future Life Progression (FLP) or Future Progression is a branch of hypnotherapy that can provide insight into further along your current life path. You will normally discuss beforehand what area it is you wish to explore, so that the hypnotherapist can lead you in that direction. However, the subconscious mind will be at play, so the most relevant information for you in your current reality will likely come forth. To exemplify, you may be asking about finding love again and try focusing purely on this, but the subconscious mind will want you to examine another area of your life that is creating a block, such as your grief.

FLP is not only limited to this life, but can also take you into your next life or future lives, even if you do not believe in the afterlife or reincarnation. You do not need to believe in past life or a future life for it to be effective, you just need to believe in yourself enough to want to reach your highest potential, and clear all aspects of life that are holding you back.

FLP gives you the opportunity to make the choices needed to live the life you choose. We make choices each and every day, whether to have tea or coffee, a good day or a bad day, and each of these choices shapes our future. FLP can reveal potential options and help you to move forward from your current reality, one which may feel stuck or overwhelming.

I would suggest that if you are a visual person undergoing this therapy, if you could not see anything in your future, you may fear the worst. However, in reality, it could simply be blank as sight is not your strongest sense, you are an analytical person, or you are struggling to see the way forward in your waking life. If you are uncomfortable with hypnosis, you could try guided meditation for future progression (rather than future life), but once again, I would recommend this practice if you are more of a visual person.

Genealogy

Genealogy is the study of our families, family history and lineage which I have seen many families undertake following the death of their loved ones. When families had listened to their loved one's stories in the last months and weeks of their life, they had learned untold or forgotten stories of their ancestors, and in turn, learned more about their families and themselves. The family who were left behind were connected through the passion and intrigue of learning more about their loved one and their lineage, and found it both a welcome distraction and healing too.

You can discover more about your family storytelling, interviews, and through online searches of records or genealogy specific websites. Children can also become involved with the family tree process, looking through old photos and learning how their ancestors helped shape the history of your world and the world at large.

Goal Setting

I am an advocate for goal setting at any time in our life, but believe it is even more significant during times of loss, where we can feel demotivated and cannot imagine the next step forward. During emotive and challenging times, choose to either write down your largest life goal and start to note down small steps you undertake, or start small and set a goal for the day ahead. Whatever your mindset can cope with, work with that, as setting attainable goals is key in the process. You may find it helpful to give each month in the calendar a specific goal such as healing, decluttering, or courage. Think of an achievable timeframe for your task, and do not be afraid to include others to help support you in achieving your goal, whether it is asking them to help with food shopping or to being a companion on your trip of a lifetime.

Goal setting helps aid self-confidence, motivation, life meaning, greater focus, memory recall, a creative process that takes us away from distractions, as well as creating a document of our intentions, that helps with our motivation and accountability of seeing our wishes come to fruition.

When writing down goals, write in a positive fashion with action-focused statements, as positive words start to rewire the brain to think differently. If you are finding it difficult to compile a list of your goals or wishes, use this time to sit and be with your thoughts, and reflect on what is happening for you and write down these words instead. If on the other hand you are loving the idea of goal setting, you may wish to look further into the chapters Life Coaching and Time Management Techniques.

Gratitude

When we are experiencing life after loss, it is easier to focus on what we do not have rather than what we do have. This naturally shifts our energy to the negative viewpoint of what is missing in our life, rather than on a positive of all the wonderful things that remain. It may seem like an oxymoron that I am coupling gratitude with grief, but gratitude is like many of the tools within this book – they require practice until you begin to realise the value in them.

Start with one grateful statement today, maybe when you first wake in the morning and see the sun shining outside, the soothing warmth of a cup of tea, or seeing a rainbow as a sign of hope.

As you begin to feel more comfortable around gratitude in your grief, you can start the day with three to five things you are grateful for and add in why you are grateful for them. For example, "I am grateful for my home as it provides shelter and safety as I continue to heal each and every day."

You may like to try a physical practice by using a gratitude stone. This simple bedtime ritual is holding a stone or crystal that has a sentimental meaning to you, and reflecting back on the happiest moments of the day. You could start a gratitude journal or jar, where you note down your moments of gratefulness. In addition – or as its own practice – you can end your day by giving gratitude through your voice by saying all the positives from the day. You could say them to a loved one, the Universe, or whatever connection which brings you the greatest comfort.

Guided Vision Therapy

Guided Vision Therapy, also known as guided image therapy or guided visualisation, is used for a variety of emotional and physical conditions. This therapy has been referred to as a directed daydream, and is often used by cognitive behavioural therapists as it helps with changing the way you think about connecting with ourselves and others, both in past situations and in the future.

Visualisations can be self-taught too, through books, online, DVDs and through other interactive formats, but you may experience a deeper therapeutic effect if undertaken with a therapist, due to the hypnotherapy aspects of the tool, and you could try a guided visualisation at home if you are not drawn to talking therapies.

Havening Technique

The Havening Technique is a therapy that accesses traumatic and stressful encoding and transforms it through sensory touch and specific words, positively altering your thoughts, feelings, perception, mood, and behaviour.

Havening, the transitive verb of the word haven, means to put into a safe place, and so this psychosensory approach works well with phobias, physical aches and pains, past memories and events, and emotions such as anger, fear, embarrassment, or grief.

Havening Technique can be experienced with a practitioner, who will gently but repeatedly touch key points on your hands, arms, and face. If you would feel uncomfortable with this, you could undertake the touch elements yourself with the practitioner present, or undertake self-Havening techniques by accessing videos online.

Homeopathy

Homeopathy is a vibrational energy system that stimulates the body into creating its own healing processes. Homeopathy or homeopathic medicine is obtained through extremely small quantities of nanoparticles of substances extracted from plants, animals or minerals. The remedies are so diluted that, based on chemistry, it is difficult to find molecules of the original substance in the remedies. Homeopathy is based on the principle of "like treats like", where a substance that causes symptoms when taken in large doses can be used in small amounts to treat the symptom. A homeopath will prescribe homeopathic medicines based on your presenting symptoms and overall health.

Hypnotherapy and Self-Hypnosis

Hypnotherapy is a guided relaxation to a state of focused attention and increased suggestibility to access the subconscious mind to help you deal with issues in your life. The use of hypnotherapy in grief is so successful because it works with the subconscious mind, home of our embedded thoughts, beliefs and behaviours, and so can help you understand your loss from a new perspective. Hypnotherapy can reduce grief duration and intensity, reconnect with positive memories, motivate you to move forwards without guilt, reduce stress, anxiety, depression and insomnia, as well as reducing physical signs and symptoms such as loss of appetite, overeating, or nausea and sickness.

Self-hypnosis is another option which can be experienced through an appropriate audio format such as CD, MP3 download, or online resource. Whilst this guidebook uses the word grief, many self-hypnosis resources tend to use alternative terms such as bereavement and loss, overcoming bereavement or hypnotherapy for loss.

Hypnotherapy is a tool for personal growth but is not suitable for everyone. It is advisable to consult your usual healthcare practitioner prior to commencing hypnotherapy work. In addition, there are contraindications for hypnotherapy (although practitioners vary in the client choice), and many do not work with severe psychological disorders, highly-medicated individuals, or anyone under the influence of recreational drugs or alcohol.

Indian Head Massage

Indian head massage (also known as champissage) is an ancient practice which works with the marma points (similar to acupressure points) through massage.

Indian head massage is believed to aid relaxation, relieve tension, aches and pains, remove toxins, and reduce sinus congestion, eye pain, headaches, stress, and insomnia. It can also stimulate blood circulation, scalp and hair growth, boost the immune system, encourage lymph drainage, and the elimination of toxins and waste.

Indian Head Massage can be carried out seated or on a treatment couch, and involves being massaged over your upper back, shoulders, arms, neck, head, ears and face for approximately thirty minutes.

Please note that there are some contraindications, including head or neck injuries, heart conditions which include low or high blood pressure, high temperature, history of deep vein thrombosis, infectious diseases, influenza, intoxication or drug use, migraines (during attack), osteoporosis, recent haemorrhage, and scalp or skin infections.

Inner Child Work and Current Life Regression

We all have our own life story which is formulated by the past history of our environment, life events, and connections. In our childhood, we sustain damage of who we once were, from a small event of having one of our drawings screwed up and thrown away, through to being subjected to abuse. We all carry our own individual stories and invisible scars.

Inner child work is how we find, reconnect, understand, and heal our dissociated, fragmented and wounded parts of our younger self; our inner child. When we reconnect and process our wounds, we understand and release our fears, phobias, pains, and the source of where it all began.

When we experience trauma in our life, both a body memory and an emotional memory are formed. So, whilst you are currently with your grief, your body will be holding body and emotional memories from past losses, such as losing a toy in childhood or a broken relationship in your teen years, which can consolidate your current physical and emotional state.

Inner child work is useful for those who have unresolved issues from their childhood and younger years, and are no longer able to openly discuss with the deceased and carry unfinished business in their heart, body, and mind, especially with issues such as abandonment or abuse.

Inner child work is not light work, and you will need to advise your healthcare professional before undertaking the process. Inner child work encourages you to face past events, so courage and determination are required as you may need to deal with past losses, as well as current loss, possibly resulting in doubling your grief emotions. However, it does not have to be a self-help tool, and a qualified hypnotherapist or regression therapist will support you through the processes. It is often noted that once you have experienced an initial catharsis, the recovery and healing is far quicker compared to leaving your past and grief unaccessed.

Whilst many therapists will have their own way of working, one of the most commonly-used frameworks of inner child work comes from the works of John Bradshaw. Bradshaw proffered six themes: trust, validation, shock and anger, sadness, remorse, and loneliness. Inner child work can be heavy but there are some gentler exercises you may wish to read through or try.

Speak to your inner child

Acknowledge your inner child and speak to them in the utmost love, kindness and respect. Either in a meditative state, or from talking to yourself in a mirror, say nurturing words to your younger self. For example: "I hear you. I'm sorry. I forgive you. I love you."

Letter writing

The power of pen to paper connection is often undervalued, so try to write a letter to your younger self. What do you understand now as your older self? What one piece of advice would you give to your younger self?

You may choose to write a letter to the perpetrator in your life, whether they are still on earth or deceased. Write down all the words you want to tell them; no matter how crass or angry, let it all flow out on to the pages. You may wish to burn the letter at the end and release it out into the world or bury the ashes in the earth to be transmuted into positivity. In whatever way you need to seek closure of these released words, go with that.

Photographs

Find a time when you will not be disturbed, and look through your old photographs. What memories come up for you? What do you sense from this snapshot in time?

Playtime

What did you love to do as a child? Play with bricks, build a den, colouring, paddling in a pool, eating your favourite food? Allow yourself to indulge in your happier childhood memories for one day.

Meditation

Inner child guided meditations are readily available on the Internet and mobile phone apps, and can be gentle enough to be undertaken on your own. Allow a time for gentleness after the meditation and drink plenty of water too.

Movement

A great way to release and move our emotions on is through movement, and yoga is particularly beneficial and healing in emotional matters, so access inner child yoga exercises online.

Your inner child is a true part of who you are today, so allow yourself the time, energy, emotions, and resources to start reconnecting with the lost parts of you, so that you can feel whole once again.

The main difference between Inner Child Work and Current Life Regression (CLR) is that CLR is used to address the original source of an issue that is believed to have occurred in the post childhood years. Whilst CLR is a stand-alone therapy, from my personal practitioner experience, it inevitably seems to go back to the childhood years once the client starts to connect with their earlier memories and energies.

Iridology

Iridology (also known as iridodiagnosis or iridiagnosis) is the study of our health through examining patterns, colours, and characteristics of the iris, the coloured part of our eye. There is a Chinese proverb: "A poor doctor cures; a good doctor prevents," and this is the theory of iridology. An Iridologist can determine if any of our systems, organs or glands are overactive, inflamed, or distressed, before they even start to produce any signs or symptoms. By detecting imbalance and acting accordingly before the dis-ease occurs, whether it is adjustments to our dietary intake, lifestyle, or environment.

Please ensure you find a reputable and registered iridologist and do not attempt to self-diagnose.

Journaling

Journaling is a written record of our thoughts and feelings

which forms a record of personal awareness, growth and transformation. Ideally journals should be completed daily, but as always, do what feels right for you and do not force your writing for the sake of a daily entry. In times of grief, some may refer to journaling as a grief diary or grief journal.

Benefits of journaling include reduced stress and anxiety, insight into our triggers and coping mechanisms, identifying negative thought and behaviour patterns, and seeing our thoughts and feelings laid bare enables us to prioritise our life.

The best way in which to start journaling is like anything; simply start. Treat yourself to a notebook that resonates with you, and is purely for the purpose of journaling. Some people like a black book for doodling and sticking memorabilia in, some like a page-a-day diary, and others just a lined notepad. Go for what suits your creative style and intention for use.

Your journaling will be most effective if you do it daily for about around twenty minutes, whether that is as you rise up in the morning, during your lunch break, or a reflection at the end of the day. Whilst you may wish to start a grief journal at this time, there are other types of journaling which may also help you with moving forward or for specific areas of your life: art, bullet, dream, exercise, food, garden, gratitude, idea, pocket, poetry, prayer, pregnancy, project, reading, reflective, time capsule, travel, and writing journaling.

There are many online resources for journaling inspiration, from free downloads to examples on Pinterest, if you need a little help starting your creative process.

Journey Work

Journey Work, also known as The Journey or Journey Therapy was developed by Brandon Bays. It is a guided technique designed to help access forgotten or repressed memories and emotions that are negatively impacting on our physical and emotional well-being. Through accessing the original source, one is able to address the dis-ease or emotional shutdown and begin a healing process.

After an initial discussion of your specific needs with the Journey practitioner, the Journey process starts with what is referred to as the drop-through. This investigates and locates the memories or emotions that have been forgotten or suppressed. The next step, the campfire, is about free and authentic speech from the part of the body where the repression is felt. This leads to exploring what resources would have helped in the past event, and this insight is then used to positively transform the old issue into a new positive. The final part is called future pace, where you experience the outcome of the new positive integration of the Journey Work.

Journey Work sessions run for the time needed to access and address the memories and emotions, so tend to be over two hours in length. People have likened Journey Work to neuro-linguistic programming but with a greater emphasis on spirituality.

Kinesiology

Kinesiology is a therapy that uses muscle monitoring (biofeedback) to detect and correct imbalances that may relate to stress, nutrition or injury, and can be useful in past and present grief. The practitioner often asks the body questions silently so we cannot logically answer the questions, so the muscle-testing technique reveals our truth and new insight into our conscious awareness. This enables us to understand matters from a new perspective which we may otherwise have chosen to deny, hide or avoid.

Laughter Yoga Therapy

The old adage tells us that "laughter is the best medicine", and this may just be the case with laughter yoga therapy. This alternative type of yoga is effective in grief, based around the theory that deep belly laughs release endorphins (our feel-good chemicals), release repressed emotions, and reduce feelings of stress and anxiety.

Laughter and humour have a place in palliative care, death, and life itself, but whilst you may feel it is inappropriate, and feel unable to attend a class as a griever, you can access lessons online so you can undertake this alternative yoga in your own space by searching the Internet for sessions.

Life Between Life

Earlier we discussed Life Between Life (LBL) in the chapter The In-Between States, where we learned how this branch of hypnotherapy regresses us back to our soul's existence between your immediate past life and your current incarnation. LBL can address specific objectives, such as your life purpose and the life lessons you chose to learn for your highest good in this current life. LBL has a place in grief recovery in that it can bring you a deeper understanding of why you had to experience your current loss from a soul perspective, and it may well be pertaining to your loved one's own life lessons too.

Beyond the ego-led questions of why life is how it is right now, LBL can provide insight into your soul path, and discover which creative or spiritual tools to develop or enhance for your soul's highest purpose in this life.

Life Coaching

A life coach is a therapist that helps motivate and empower you to create and meet the goals, needs, and outcomes you wish to have in your life, whether the area of your life is personal development, spirituality, health, relationships or career. Together you identify your current situation, attitudes, beliefs, and barriers, and together set suitable goals for positive change.

If life coaching does not seem right for you at this particular point in time, consider Grief Coaching. These coaches work specifically with the grieving, aiming to help you utilise your coping strategies and inner resources, and set goals around relationships and interests that can bring greater meaning back into your life.

Mantras

A mantra is a word, statement or sound that is repeated either through being spoken, chanted, whispered, or repeated in the mind. Mantras are believed to help clear your consciousness of your busy thoughts, to make room for a positive idea or intention.

You can work with an ancient Sanskrit mantra or a simple sentence, and it is believed in order to reap the greatest benefit, the mantra should be repeated 108 times in one instance, which you can count through using mala beads. Mantras are a great way to start the day, and it is suggested that they are used for thirty days for optimal effect.

You will know that a mantra is right for you when it is meaningful, and produces positive feelings such as self-love or confidence. Here are some examples of Sanskrit and simple mantras but working with words that are key to your grief healing are important factors, so feel free to create your own.

Eem Hreem Kleem: I radiate confidence and strength.

Om Durgaya Namah: I am fearless.

Samprati Hum: My true self is wide awake.

Shree Gum Namah: My limitless awareness overcomes all obstacles.

Sheevo Hum: I am pure potentiality.

I am strong enough to fully embrace my grief.

I heal my past by being fully in the present in this moment.

I turn to love instead of loss.

I choose to see my grief as an opportunity for optimal growth.

Meaning

Elisabeth Kübler-Ross wrote about the five stages of grief, and co-authored *On Grief and Grieving* with David Kessler. Kessler went on to write *Finding Meaning: The Sixth Stage of Grief* where he said, "meaning comes through finding a way to sustain your love for the person after their death while you're moving forward with your life."

Viktor E. Frankl, holocaust survivor, neurologist and psychiatrist, believed the meaning of life could be found in every moment of living even in suffering and death. Frankl understood meaning to come from three sources: purposeful work, love, and courage in the face of adversity.

When you search for the lessons of death and grief, you are actively choosing to move forward as a survivor and even a thriver, rather than remaining a victim. You can transcend pain by searching for meaning, which can lead to opportunities for growth and transformation. You will change with grief, but you can choose to have a positive transformation, and whilst it may not be an easy path forward, it is a way forward.

How can you begin to find meaning? Some find comfort through their religious and spiritual beliefs, others from their loved one being a donor and gifting their life to another, whilst some, when faced with their own mortality, fervently commit to living more fully.

Take time to consider what your life's meaning could be, possibly starting with Frankl's three categories: purposeful work, love, and courage until your own inspirational words come:

Purposeful Work

- Consider learning a new skill or undertaking a career change to pursue your dreams
- Volunteer for a heartfelt cause
- Start a fundraiser
- Simplify your career for a better work-life balance

Love

- Develop your connections with yourself, friends, family, colleagues, and the world around you
- What one thing you have always loved to do or longed to do?

Courage

- Allow yourself to grieve authentically, no bars held
- Consider joy and playfulness as a daily activity
- List what is really important to you in your life. What can you discard?
- Share your message with others, be it on social media or writing a book
- Plan that trip you always wanted to take and see it through
- Rethink your attitude and beliefs around dying and death

Meditation

Be open to allowing yourself to learn new ways to change your busy or negative thoughts, in order to create a clearer path ahead. When you immerse yourself in the right meditation, it can be like a plug has been pulled out of your brave face persona bringing about a much-needed release.

In meditation you may be able to connect to yourself, a colour, guide, energy, or loved one. On one level or another there will be a connection, one where we can gain knowledge, insight, relaxation, comfort or meaning. Meditation can help us develop a supportive lament in our life that prevents us from hitting rock bottom.

If you are new to meditation, you can simply start by sitting comfortably for two minutes and focusing on your breath coming in and out of your body. You could say, "Breathing in, breathing out," in your mind so that you are not so easily distracted by your thoughts. What also works well for beginners are guided meditations, where you will be specifically guided through the meditation, with both a voice and command to focus on.

As we have already learned, a meditation can be to connect with angels, animals, archangels, Ascended Masters, colours, deities, or chakras. There is a meditation for everything from anxiety and grief, through to creating abundance or better quality sleep. Meditations are free to access through online resources and mobile apps, but do listen to a few seconds of the meditation before settling down, as the music choice, teacher's voice, or pace of guidance can be off-putting, and may not be the most suitable choice for you.

Meditations can be further enhanced through finding a comfortable and sustainable sitting or lying position, burning incense, lighting a candle, holding a crystal, or creating subdued lighting.

Memory Box

A memory box (or bereavement box) is a collection of items that remind you of your loved one and your shared moments. Memory boxes can be started whilst people are still alive, as well as following their death, and are therapeutic grief work with children and young adults when their family are terminally ill or deceased.

The box can be any size from a small trinket right up to a full-sized storage box, with contents that are unique to you and your memories, such as:

- Photographs
- Jewellery
- Books
- Diaries
- Letters, cards and postcards
- Certificates and awards

- Medals and rosettes
- Items of clothing
- Toys and ornaments
- Lock of hair
- Memorabilia such as shells, drawings, ticket stubs

You can start a new jar or box from this day forward, where you save cinema tickets, travel tickets, pressed flowers, or little notes with happy dates and achievements on.

Metamorphic Technique

Practitioners of the Metamorphic Technique state it is not a therapy as they are not manipulating you in any way, and rather that it is a stand-alone technique. The method involves lightly stroking points on the feet, hands and head which are said to correspond with our time in the womb, where behaviour patterns and challenges first begin.

Practitioners cannot predict the session's outcome, as it is held that any transformation manifests purely from within the recipient. Metamorphic Technique practitioners say the technique is safe from babies to the elderly, but is particularly beneficial during challenging times, such as loss and grief.

Mindfulness

Mindfulness is about living and accepting everything in the now, as when we focus all our attention and senses in the current moment, we discover the truth of what really is in the now, and are not thinking of the past or future. One of the key concepts of mindfulness is the practice of returning back to the now, even if you don't like what you find. Whilst returning will not change the reality you can change your relationship with it, in that it can become less overwhelming or beyond your control.

Mindfulness' other key concepts include: non-judgment (allowing things to be without questioning or changing them), acceptance (it is what it is), beginner's mind (viewing everything as a new experience), trust (trusting your intuition and having faith that everything is going to be okay), patience (you can only be where you are so be present and patient) and gratitude.

Mindfulness acknowledges we cannot achieve all of these key concepts overnight but we can start to search for the positive opportunities in this present moment. Start to notice moments where you can be more mindful by slowing down and bringing everything back to the now, such as brushing your teeth, looking out of a window, drinking your coffee, eating a meal, starting up your computer, having a shower, emptying the dishwasher, brushing your hair, entering the workplace, or being stuck in traffic. These recurring daily activities are undertaken in auto-pilot mode rather than being fully present so allow yourself to be mindful of these moments that make up your day, week, and life.

You know what else we do daily? Breathe. Take a minute to observe your breathing. Breathe in and out as you normally would but notice the time between each inhalation and exhalation. When your mind wanders, gently bring your attention back to your breath. If you wish to work more with your awareness of breath, here are a few exercises for you to try.

One Breath Out, One Breath In
Pause and follow your out-breath all the way out in awareness, and then follow your in-breath all the way in.

7/11 Breathing
Breathe in whilst you count to 7, and breathe out whilst you count to 11.

Box Breathing
This breathwork positively impacts on our parasympathetic nervous system, the system that helps to calm the body and reduces stress hormones' production.

- Breathe in for the count of 4
- Hold for 4
- Breathe out for 4
- Hold for 4
- Repeat this cycle until you are aware of the present moment and your breath.

Five Senses Exercise

This exercise brings your awareness back to your immediate environment and experiences it with each of your five senses.

Follow this order to practise the Five Senses Exercise:

Sight: Look around you and bring your attention to five things you can see. Pick something that you don't normally notice, like a shadow or a small crack in the concrete.

Touch: Bring awareness to four things you can feel, like the texture of your clothes, the breeze on your skin, or the smooth surface of a table you are resting your hands on.

Hearing: Take a moment to listen to three things in the background, such as birdsong, refrigerator humming, or the faint sounds of traffic nearby.

Smell: Bring your awareness to smells, whether they're pleasant or unpleasant. Perhaps the outdoor breeze carrying a whiff of nature, or the smell of a fast food restaurant.

Taste: Focus on one thing that you can taste right now. You can take a sip of a drink, chew a piece of gum, eat something, or even open your mouth to search the air for a taste.

As always, I am all for breaking positive changes down into bite-sized steps, so you may prefer these quicker tools:

Tune In: Just stop and listen to what you can hear here at this moment, and listen without judgement or analysis. A clock ticking, a car driving by, birds, wind blowing.

A Colour A Day: Choose a colour at the start of each day, and throughout your day, begin to notice objects in that colour.

Hang On A Minute: Find a watch or clock with a second

hand, and count back from 60.

This is good for being in the moment as well as pandering to your inner child needs.

Weather Watching: Cloud watching, looking at the raindrops rolling down a window, even catching raindrops or snowflakes on your tongue, doing a rain dance, making a wish on a rainbow.

Mother Nature

When we are stripped of a sense of security in life, we can draw comfort from the certainty of Mother Nature and the seasons. Spring can bring hope as buds remind us of new beginnings and a time of manifestation and rest before we bloom. Summer is a time of lightness and high energies. Autumn is a time to soften and quieten as we move into Winter where we are encouraged to shed what no longer serves us.

Whilst you may feel like permanently hibernating, Mother Nature can serve as a healer, with her sun rising every morning denoting a new day of opportunities, and the Moon's gentler energy lighting our way in the darker hours. Stepping outdoors each day can be so beneficial just by listening to the wind, feeling grounded by gardening, energised from the warmth of the sun, or cleansed by the coolness of the rain. Mother Nature and her natural cycles encourage us to embrace our innate ability to constantly grow, release and rebirth. No longer must we wait for an expected "one day", but rather start to create daily rituals from today. As each season passes, we will see a new version of ourselves with our own unique positive changes.

If you feel overwhelmed by going out, bring Mother Nature to you with an indoor sun or moon altar, growing plants and herbs on a windowsill, or creating a miniature zen or fairy garden. If you are an outdoors type of person, look into joining a gardening or allotment group, participating in nature therapies like forest or meadow bathing, or booking a break in a natural setting such as woodlands or lakeside.

Mudras

The word Mudra comes from a Sanskrit word meaning seal, mark or gesture, and refers to symbolic gestures made with the hands and fingers. The Mudra theory holds that each digit represents an element – the thumb represents fire, the index finger air, the middle finger ether or space, the ring finger earth and the pinkie finger for water. Mudras are used in yoga and meditation, but can be used alone as an energy tool which can be subtly used as you go about your day. Different hand and finger positions channel different energy flow, both within the body and our subtle bodies, the energetic bodies outside of our physical body. Mudras are best practised for between two and ten minutes a day as a general guideline.

There are over one hundred different mudras, but we will take a look at those that are the most closely related to grief.

Acceptance

For overcoming sadness, unnecessary resistance to situations, and being stuck in the past.

Position: Fold the index finger so it rests in the space between your thumb. Next, have your thumb touch your pinkie finger. Make sure your thumb is resting on the nail of your pinkie.

Ahamkara

For regaining self-confidence, standing up for yourself, and overcoming your fears.

Position: Fold your index finger slightly, and touch your thumb to the outside of your index finger, a little less than halfway down. Try to keep your other fingers straight.

Apan

For a boost of energy.

Position: Touch your thumb to your middle and ring finger. Keep your pinkie and index finger as straight as possible.

Buddhi (or Bhudy)

For mental clarity and clear communication, whether internal or external dialogue.

Position: Touch your thumb to your pinkie finger, while holding your other three fingers straight.

Ganesha

For relieving obstacles in your life, regaining positivity, and courage during challenging times.

Position: Focus on your heart centre as you place your left hand in front of your chest with your palm facing outward and left thumb down. Next, place your right hand in front of your left with your right palm facing toward you and your left palm. Now, lock your fingers together in a half-bent claw position. Inhale deeply in this position and then pull outwardly on your hands as you exhale without unlocking your fingers. Repeat this motion six times, then reverse the gesture (right hand in front of your chest facing outward with the thumb down) and repeat six times.

Prana

For activating dormant energy in your body.

Position: Touch your ring and pinkie finger to the tip of your thumb, while keeping the other two fingers straight.

Rudra

For transformation, improving clarity and focus, and relieving dizziness, exhaustion and tension.

Position: Touch your thumb to your index and ring fingers while keeping your other two fingers as straight as you can.

Shuni (or Shoonya)

Healing: For staying in the present in the moment, intuition, alertness, and evoking patience and understanding.

Position: Touch the top of the middle finger and thumb together, while keeping the other three fingers straight and relaxed.

Music and Sound

Music is all around us if we only choose to listen, be it the internal sound of our heart beating, or external sounds of children laughing. Music is easily accessible and a powerful healer, from listening to "our song" and feeling nostalgic, singing at the top of your voice, playing an instrument, or attending a concert. Music can serve as an external expression of internal state through tonalities, lyrics, tempo, breathwork and movement.

There are many genres and lyrics all telling different stories, so you could choose to listen to some of the suggested songs below, or create your own playlist which could be nostalgic songs, apt lyrics, or uplifting tunes to help motivate you.

Songs on the subject of loss

Angel by Sarah McLachlan

Angels Among Us by Alabama

Ascension by Zen Music Garden

Barber's *Adagio for Strings*

Beam Me Up by Pink

Bird River Grove by Can't Hang

Brick by Ben Folds Five

Candle in the Wind by Elton John

Dance with My Father by Luther Vandross

Dancing in the Sky by Dani and Lizzy

Dog Years by Maggie Rogers

Don't Take the Girl by Tim McGraw

Esperar Pra Ver by Poolside

Fire and Rain by James Taylor

Fly by Celine Dion

For Good from *Wicked*

From Where You Are by Lighthouse
Gone Too Soon by Daughtry
Hallelujah by Jeff Buckley
Heaven by Beyoncé
Heaven Needed You More by Mikalene Ipson
Holes in the Floor of Heaven by Steve Wariner
How Can I Help You Say Goodbye by Patty Loveless
If Heaven Wasn't So Far Away by Justin Moore
I'll Be Missing You by Faith Evans and Puff Daddy
I Miss You by Avril Lavigne
In Loving Memory by Alter Bridge
Into the Fire by Bruce Springsteen
I Will Remember You by Sarah McLachlan
Let It Be by The Beatles
Lullabye by Billy Joel
Midnight Souls Still Remain by M83
Missing You by Diana Ross
My Heart Will Go On by Celine Dion
Never Forget You by Mariah Carey
Nobody Knows by Tony Rich Project
Not as We by Alanis Morissette
Now You Belong To Heaven by Mari Olsen
Nuvole Bianche by Ludovico Einaudi
One More Day by Diamond Rio
One Sweet Day by Mariah Carey and Boyz II Men
Only Time by Enya
Only To Be With You by Judah & the Lion
Over the Rainbow by Israel Kamakawiwo'ole
Rescue by Lauran Daigle
Rise Up by Andra Day
See You Again by Wiz Khalifa ft. Charlie Puth
Showboat by Boombox
Small Bump by Ed Sheeran
Stars by Grace Potter & The Nocturnals

Suaimhneas by Ceilidh

Sunshine by Matisyahu

Tears in Heaven by Eric Clapton

The Day She Fell To Earth by The Buffseeds

The River by Kat Wright

The Scientist by Coldplay

Think of Me by Jackie Evancho

Three Little Birds by Bob Marley

'Till It Happens To You by Lady Gaga

Upside Down by Jack Johnson

Wake Me Up When September Ends by Green Day

What a Wonderful World by Israel Kamakawiwo'ole

When I Get Where I'm Going by Brad Paisley & Dolly Parton

When I See You Again by Emerson Drive

When Tomorrow Starts Without Me by Stephen Meara-Blount

Who You'd Be Today by Kenny Chesney

Wishing You Were Somehow Here Again from *The Phantom of the Opera*

You Are Not Alone by Michael Jackson

You Can Let Go Now Daddy by Patricia Macguire

You Get What You Give by New Radicals

You'll Be In My Heart by Phil Collins

You Raise Me Up by Secret Garden

Sound has been with us since the beginning of time, with the first spoken sacred word believed to be OM (Ohm or Aum) as well as our first experience in the beginning of our own life being the sound of our mother's heartbeat in the womb. Sound Therapy, also known as sound healing, combines therapeutic techniques (rhythm, instruments and voice) to influence our physiological, neurological and psychological well-being, which helps restore and rebalance our physical and emotional health.

You can experience sound healing with a practitioner in local communities, often advertised as a gong or sound bath, which incorporate gongs, drums, bells, Tibetan or crystal quartz singing bowls, tuning forks, tingshas (small Tibetan cymbals), and voice. Each practitioner will be unique, so if one does not resonate with you, do try another. If you wish to experience sound healing at home you can listen to sound healing, binaural sounds or Theta waves music, or even create your own through chanting, singing, and voicing positive affirmations aloud.

If you wish to purchase bells, tingshas or singing bowls, you can use them by striking the instrument and circling it around your body from your head to your feet, whilst envisaging the sound vibrations shattering your negative emotions. You can also clear rooms, homes and boundaries, by striking the instrument in every corner of every room, working in a clockwise direction, until the entire room or home is cleansed through vibrations.

Chanting

Chanting is when we say or shout repeatedly in a sing-song tone and you can start with simple sounds, such as OM or AH.

OM

OM is a sacred sound and is connected to our seventh chakra, the crown chakra.

- Take a deep breath in, and as you exhale, chant the sound OM.
- Allow the breath to fully empty, and then breathe in again and repeat the chant.
- Continue this cycle at your own breath pace, and repeat for two minutes, or until it feels intuitively right for you.

AH

The sound AH is a high-pitched sound like "ma" and is located in the Heart chakra.

- Take a deep breath in, and as you exhale the same chant Aaa-Uuu-Mmm.
- You are aiming to feel the "Aaa" sound in your belly, "Uuu" in your chest, and the "Mmm" in your head.
- Breathe in again and continue at your own pace for two minutes, or until it feels intuitively right for you.

If you are aware of carrying a heaviness in a certain part of your body, refer back to the Chakras chapter where each chakra had an associated sound listed.

Naturopathic Medicine

Naturopathic medicine is a holistic system that uses natural remedies to rebalance the body's energies so that it can heal itself. Drawing on both traditional treatments and modern science, remedies include acupuncture, exercise, homeopathy and massage which we have looked at as stand-alone therapies. Naturopathic medicine may be for you if you are not sure what you need, as there is a thorough one to two hour initial health assessment to determine your needs and plan accordingly.

Neuro-Linguistic Programming

Neuro-linguistic programming (NLP) is a psychological approach that uses a variety of perceptual, behavioural, and communication techniques to change non-conducive thoughts and actions. Techniques include Anchoring (turning sensory experiences into a trigger), rapport (the NLP practitioner matches your physical behaviour to improve communication and empathy), swish pattern (rapidly replacing a learned negative with a positive), and visual and kinaesthetic dissociation (removing negatives associated with a past event).

Nutrition

When we are touched by grief it is common to experience

decision fatigue, when even making choices about what to eat can seem strenuous, and you end up opting not to eat at all, or go for the quickest and easiest option which is often unhealthy.

Nutrition may be one of the last thoughts whilst your grief is eating away at you, but stress and trauma give way to our tendency to either overeat or under-eat when life deviates from our norm. It is common for us to use alcohol to anaesthetise, drink caffeine for fuel, or eat high carbohydrate or sugary foods for ease and comfort. All of these choices will inevitably have a short-lived effect, so we need to consider trying healthier options:

- Write a meal plan for the week ahead so you know what needs doing each day at a time.
- Prepare fruit and vegetable sticks and other healthy grabbable snacks.
- People like to have a purpose, so ask them to help with meals, recipes, and shopping.
- Batch cook meals that can be frozen for future home-made microwave meals.
- One day a week use cooking as a healing and creative process with all the different colours, scents, flavours and textures.
- Drink plenty of water as caffeine, alcohol, and crying can all lead to dehydration.
- If you do not feel up to eating, try nutritious drinks instead: milkshakes, fruit juice, fruit smoothies, soups, or milky hot drinks.
- Grief and its stressful impact can lend us to being more vulnerable to physical dis-ease so keep taking your regular prescribed medications to help form a stable foundation.
- Check with your healthcare professional about undertaking a daily multivitamin whilst your dietary intake may deviate from its norm.

- Be aware of what specific emotions are triggering your overeating, as this could be indicative of you avoiding a certain emotion. Rather than trying to self-soothe through food, allow the emotions to come up and take time to fully experience them.
- Do not eat during mindless tasks such as watching television, instead take time to mindfully eat.
- Tryptophan-rich foods contain serotonin which can help regulate our moods, so try adding bananas, cheese, chicken, eggs, fish, fruit, milk, nuts, seeds, soy, spinach, tofu, turkey into your food choices.
- Review your previous dietary choices to see if you were eating foods your loved ones liked. You may wish to have an overhaul and create your own choices, be it ketogenic, paleo, gluten free, carnivore, raw, vegetarian or vegan diet.

Oracle Cards

Unlike straight-talking Tarot cards with their seventy-eight cards, oracle cards can come in various deck sizes, shapes, and themes. Oracle cards can be used in several ways depending on your needs, depending on whether you want a little daily boost or wish to use them for introspection or divination.

There are thousands of different themed oracle cards available so go with the ones you are drawn to, and I mean intuitively, not by the cheapest price tag. Connect with cards that you need at this stage in your life, be it affirmations, Angels, animals, archangels, Celtic, chakras, crystals, dragons, Druids, energy, fairies, femininity, gods and goddesses, healing, love, moon, Native American, nature, Pagan, Sacred Geometry, teenage decks, or Wiccan, to give you an idea of some of the subjects available.

Oracle cards work by connecting with your energy, so you will need to put your energy into each card before you start your readings. Oracle decks will come with a guidebook on how to do this, but it is generally advised that you look at each individual card in turn before holding the deck to your heart and saying a gratitude prayer for them coming into your life.

Please note that oracle cards always connect with our most prominent and present energy, so endeavour to work with as much positive energy as you can conjure up.

Start to ask your open-ended question, such as, "What do I need to know for the day ahead?" and repeatedly ask the same question whilst you shuffle the deck. Oracle cards are a great tool for helping to develop your intuition, so I tend to simply shuffle the deck until it feels right to stop or if a card slides or jumps out. The deck guidebook will most likely have a suggested spread rather than my spiritual shuffle approach. A spread will be a set number of cards, often taken from the top of the deck, answering a question. Go with what card reading approach feels right for you as intuition is key.

Respect your cards and they will work well for you, so keep your cards wrapped in a silk cloth, a pouch, trinket box, or proudly display them in a place that is special for you, such as an altar. Do regularly fan your deck out and use incense or a Full Moon to cleanse them so that they continue to work with your current energy and reality.

Past Life Therapy (Past Life Regression)

As we discovered in the chapter The In-Between States, PLR is when hypnotherapy is used to access past lives and the memories and experiences within these previous incarnations.

PLR can be highly effective when we are grieving as our emotions are heightened and raw, enabling us to tap in more readily to our subconscious mind and its database of past life knowledge. In our waking life, we have moments where we feel that grief and its presentations are more than we would logically expect to feel. It is through my PLR observations that I came to note that when we are so bereft in this life, it is linked to loss in a past life, so we are experiencing two or more grieving responses at once.

We reincarnate time and time again but often to the same soul group so that we can learn the same lesson from different perspectives. It is from our soul group that we learn that we have been killed, saved, loved, estranged, betrayed and heartbroken by loved ones in a previous life, and are now experiencing the same emotional resonance, hence doubling our grief responses in our current reality.

PLR can help heal elements of your current grief, as well as previous grief from accessing and positively transforming past life losses. It is imperative that you find a reputable regression therapist to help you through these timelines, and not just a past life regressionist who can take you to the event but not be able to metamorphose the life lessons.

Permission to Grieve

You could choose to buy various presents for yourself or succumb to vices to help you through your grief journey, but the greatest gift you can give yourself is the permission to grieve. We all grieve, that is one of the connections between all of us as human beings, so do not feel obligated to push your grief down for the sake of others. Give yourself permission to grieve.

Why do I use the word permission? It is because we can think about how we will do things in life, but it is taking action that manifests the greatest changes, and permission is the first step in creating shifts. You are not thinking about how you should be seen to be grieving, you are taking action to authentically grieve your way, be it screaming into a pillow or a carefree night out with friends. All grief responses are valid so I am imploring you to give yourself permission to grieve, however it feels for you. When you allow yourself to soften into your grief, others around you may soften too, as they come to understand where you are at in your grief, whether sobbing or singing.

Some of you may feel uncomfortable by joyous suggestions in grief, but modern research shows how joy and relief are as likely as anger or sadness, and can lead us to a new sense of meaning in our life, even if it is not the life we foresaw or wished for. Grief is unique in every single aspect but the only way to get through grief is to grieve. However grief presents to you, authentically connect with it without the need to justify yourself to others.

Remember:

- Grief has no timeline so take the time you need, be it days or years.
- Set aside ten minutes a day to be with your grief and accept whatever comes, whether it is smiles or tears.
- Let go of what no longer serves you, be it hobbies, negative behaviour, or people.
- Life will never be the same after loss but it can still be good.
- Say no to others and yes to yourself.

By taking ten minutes a day to sit with your grief, you will start to sense what it is that you need to start releasing; whether it is tears, words, clutter, or limiting beliefs. Trust what comes as you know yourself better than anyone else does, deep down inside. I know you may think you have forgotten who you truly are, as you have been part of someone else's life for so long, but the answers will come when you learn to trust yourself.

Pilates

Grief can feel like we are physically injured when we are filled with aches and pains from all our emotions and sleep deprivation. Movement can help both our body and mind, even undertaking gentle exercise, such as Pilates or yoga. While the methods are different, Pilates and yoga both develop strength, balance, flexibility, and breathing techniques. Yoga tends to place a greater emphasis on relaxation, meditation, and does not usually require any equipment, whereas some Pilates can incorporate special equipment, such as the Reformer, Cadillac and Wunda Chair, or systems of pulleys and springs, handles and straps to provide either resistance or support, depending on your needs.

Simple Pilates without equipment can be undertaken in your home accessing books or online videos, or you can access classes within your local community. For those who require greater support and the implementation of equipment, check your local gymnasium and health club.

Play Therapy

As the name suggests, play therapy is therapy through play, and works well for children or adults who have lost the ability to playfully explore or express themselves. Working with a play therapist, the options of play range from movement (body play), sand play, dream play, nature play, social play, pretend play, creative play, storytelling, and vocal play. As well as healing the inner child, other benefits are optimising learning, enhancing relationships, and improving physical and emotional well-being.

Podcasts

A podcast is an episodic series of spoken word digital audio files that you can listen to on a computer, mobile phone and other devices. It is essentially a pre-recorded radio talk show, and there are thousands of genres and subjects available, with grief and loss being one of them. We know we all grieve differently, and some podcasts can cater for this. Some are aimed at children and young teens, but most are for grieving adults. Podcast hosts are as different as grief itself and include comedians, grief and trauma specialists, mediums, celebrities, doctors and nurses, spiritual healers, writers, relationship specialists, funeral directors, and mental health practitioners.

Poetry

Poetry is similar to bibliotherapy but rather than being used in conjunction with professional talking therapies, such as counselling, poetry is about creating your own cathartic works. Poetry therapy is particularly valuable in helping you articulate your emotions, thoughts and feelings from your inner world to the page, if you are not a verbal person. This creative process enables you to move from silence to speech, but of a personal, unseen, and unheard expression. Writing about our painful experiences is highly conductive to grief recovery, and poetry particularly so with its free and unstructured flow of expression. Treat yourself to a notebook specifically for your poetry, to help form a sense of sacred practice for your work. This documentation will serve you as a grief journal as when you look back on your words, you may note how your perspectives have changed.

To begin your conscious writing, simply start with one word, be it someone's name or your strongest emotion at present. Alternatively, doodle over the page, or draw a continual looping pattern over the page (like a bowl of spaghetti) until words come to you.

Polarity Therapy

Polarity Therapy is an energy healing system that enables you to look at any pain, stress and dis-ease that may be present in your body. It provides an opportunity to access and unwind the origins that create physical, mental and emotional symptoms through verbal communication and reflective listening.

Of the five elements (water, air, fire, earth and ether), Polarity Therapy believes that ether is energetically stored in our neck and throat, connecting with the specific emotions of grief. It is with this belief in mind, that Polarity Therapy practitioners open the ether centre to create flow and thereby release the grief, a healing which is not offered in conventional talking therapies. Polarity therapy incorporates techniques that harmonise ether in other elements within the body, particularly our nervous and musculoskeletal systems.

As well as the healing itself, the practitioner will use verbal skills to help you create a greater sense of awareness, reduce anxiety and stress, provide clarity and focus, relieve physical pains connected with emotional blocks, help rebalance emotions, restore vitality, increase personal power and sense of self, as well as being a resource of support during times of grief, illness, injury, or trauma.

Qigong

Qigong (pronounced chee-gung) is an ancient Chinese practice that involves meditative and physical movement exercises. These two elements have Yin and Yang aspects: Yin is being it; Yang is doing it. Yin qigong exercises are expressed through relaxed stretching, visualisation, and breathing. Yang qigong exercises are expressed in a more aerobic way, and are particularly effective on our immune system.

Exercises

Qigong is a gentler form of exercise through movements that are repeated, to both stretch and strengthen the body, enhance body awareness, improve body posture, increase blood, synovial, and lymph fluid movement, and enhance balance and proprioception.

Qigong Meditations and Visualisations

Qigong meditation is about using your mind to direct the flow of energy within your body, as it is held that controlling this energy flow is one key to good health. Qigong guided meditation visualisations are readily available through the Internet and on mobile phone apps. Qigong also incorporates the use of positive affirmations.

Breathwork

Grief is held in the lungs according to Traditional Chinese Medicine, and in Qigong, each breath is used as a metaphor, with inhalation breathing in the positive life force, and the exhale representing the letting go of something that is no longer with us, be it a person or a belonging. Qigong practitioners believe that when we learn to breathe, we can transform our life.

Qigong is suitable for many ages and abilities, and can be undertaken by yourself. Due to the vast range of exercises, meditations, and breathwork, be sure to research online to find which specific exercises you resonate with, and create your own Qigong routine.

You may also wish to look into Tai Chi, another Chinese system that works with Chi, but one that uses the opposites of Yin and Yang, by working with forward and backward, gentleness and strength, action and serenity.

Qoya

Qoya is an active movement-based practice that claims to release the body, mind and soul of any restrictions, through actively shaking each and every part of the body. Qoya is based on the idea of remembering and releasing the true essence of who we are; a wild and free being. Qoya is believed to increase energy levels, as well as banishing stress and tension by increasing the awareness of your body. If you are drawn to this wild chakra-shaking form of movement, you can access different videos online, but there are classes and retreats available too.

Resilience

Resilience is the strength and speed in which we respond and recover from adversity. When we speak about resilience in terms of loss, it is an adaptation and transition from passive mourning into actively remembering and finding meaning and purpose from the loss.

Most grief literature and advice tells of the negativity of grief, voicing how grief will never be overcome, can cause relationship breakdowns, and will generally be a painful existence. This is like many aspects of life where not only are we led to believe the worst, but often left without tools or motivation on how to handle such challenges, leading to the tendency for us to survive rather than thrive.

Information is one thing, but being passive in learning this information is quite another.

Grief is not about Kübler-Ross's stages of grief nor is it about severing all ties as Freud would have us believe. Negative literature and opinion tends to come from a viewpoint on complicated grief, and whilst complicated grief certainly exists, it only affects around 10% of us, meaning 90% can truly thrive in life after loss.

Resilience can help you navigate loss, giving you a sense of control back over your life and your journey through grief. Grief is a human experience, and as a result, we already have an in-built ability to be prepared for it, we just need to learn how to use it.

If you are on your grief journey and are moving forward, resilience could be just the tool for you.

Ask for Help and Accept It

Are there people, a job role or a purpose in your life that you feel driven to still live for? Once you accept that your loss is real, remember what was and combine the realisations with a desire to move beyond the final event of death. This is not an easy task, and emotions like guilt and fear will twang at your heartstrings, but like with Mindfulness, you do not have to like the present moment but accept it for what it is. Your emotions may be stronger than dislike and more like a yell of "I hate my life", but somewhere in your inbuilt resilience, a niggle will encourage you that you need to try and move forward, for yourself, your friends, family, and even in memory of your lost ones.

We are not looking for instant results or perfection, more a willingness to start actively participating in your life journey and not purely your grief journey. You do not even need to set a five-year plan, just functioning adequately for the next five minutes or day ahead is a good tentative step. You can still cry, yell, and be angry, resilience is not about pushing your emotions down, it is a determined mindset to undertake whatever you need to as a means to taking control of your life and the grief within it. One of the largest parts of grief is about learning how to live again in the world, even if it seems like a totally different world to the one before loss, but there ways in which we can try.

Positive Intention

We have learned about the importance of a determined mindset when setting a positive intention to connect with an angel or guide, and it is the same positive outlook needed in developing our resilience. Set a positive intention to actively be part of your purposeful grief as you attempt to move forward with purpose. You can create a positive affirmation to use every time you need a resilience boost or reminder.

Positive Search

It is during our darkest times that we are more able to see the smallest glimmer of light. When we are affected by grief, it can be challenging to focus on anything for a great length of time, so when you have moments of focus, use it to seek out the positive. Life is shaped by whether we focus on the negative or positive aspects, so when concentration is limited, always focus on the positive. Search for the good in each day, even reflect back over the day each evening. When you find the positive, acknowledge it, and you can even note it down, whether that is as a social media post, in your journal or a note around the home. Build on the positives each and every day, no matter how small they are.

Whether you opt for resilience, or another tool, trust that you will find your way through grief. Alternatively, if you are struggling with complicated grief, please do contact your healthcare professional or mental healthcare practitioner for support and guidance at this stage of grief.

Rituals

A ritual is an action that has a personal meaning and intention for you, and is performed regularly as part of your routine. Rituals can help us to connect to something greater than our solitary self, be it our culture, society, traditions, guides, or ancestors. Whilst positive thinking is a wonderful thing, it is positive action that truly creates our positive changes.

A ritual can start with you making your bed each morning as soon as you rise up. Not only will this practice prevent the temptation to crawl back into your duvet, it helps in starting to see the importance of the little things in life. Other ritual suggestions include exercise, journaling, reading or learning for half an hour each day.

There are grief rituals too, which may be a one-off occasion or on memorable days like birthdays, anniversaries, or seasonal holidays, and they may be just for you or with others grieving the same loss. This could be the gathering together, but could include lighting a special candle, eating and drinking their favourite foods, telling nostalgic stories, watching their favourite movie, creating a piece of art or text in their memory, reading inspirational words, wearing their favourite colour, playing or singing a meaningful song, looking through old photographs, visiting their grave, or planting a tree or flowers.

Seitai Therapy

The Japanese word Seitai means "to bring the body into order" which it aims to achieve by using the thumbs, fingers and elbows on acupressure points or "tsubos". It works on the principle that physical pain manifests due to underlying disharmony within the body as a result of dis-ease or trauma. Seitai therapy is based on the belief that the body is designed to heal itself, so once manipulated back into a near-optimal shape, the self-healing abilities will take care of the rest.

Developed during the last century in Japan, Seitai Therapy combines elements of Shiatsu and physical manipulation techniques deemed to be different from massage.

Self-Care

Self-care is when we deliberately undertake an activity in order to take care of our physical, emotional, mental, social and spiritual needs. Whilst it sounds simple in theory, it's something we often overlook in our lives, but more so during times of grieving, when previously simple tasks such as eating well or texting a friend can seem overwhelming or unimportant.

Whilst looking at self-care options may not seem a priority, choosing one little tool can create large shifts in our body, mind, and spirit. Start by choosing the least exhaustive or time consuming one if you wish, and when you have tried or adapted the tool into your daily routine, choose another one that appeals or seems achievable. Feel free to add in your own ideas and tasks that you are passionate about or interested in as this will motivate you. Here are some suggestions of self-care options to try:

- Allow your emotions to come and go.
- Be brave enough to fail at something new.
- Be kind to yourself.

- Be patient with yourself.
- Be creative and messy.
- Create a better work-life balance.
- Create a positive affirmation.
- Create a wish list.
- Create a sacred place in your home.
- Dance like nobody's watching.
- Declutter one cupboard.
- Do some gardening.
- Do a digital detox.
- Eat and drink well.
- Forgive yourself and others.
- Get a good night's sleep.
- Go for a walk.
- List five achievements over your lifespan.
- Make a list of stress busters.
- Meditate once a day.
- Practise breathwork.
- Read for half an hour a day.
- Respect and love your body.
- Say a prayer.
- Schedule in Me Time for at least ten minutes each and every day.
- Set clear boundaries in all your relationships.
- Sing at the top of your lungs.
- Spend time alone with your thoughts.
- Take a cleansing shower or bath.
- Volunteer in the community.
- Watch a movie.
- Write five things you are grateful for and why.

Self-Love

What is the difference between self-care and self-love? Different sources will define different things but for me, self-care is actively taking care of yourself, physically and emotionally, mental, social and spiritual needs, and self-love is loving yourself unapologetically, regardless of your physical, intellectual, emotional and social states. Whilst they are not greatly different, they are also both necessary, and together create the foundation of a happy, healthy and meaningful life.

To practise self-love, we must create a loving relationship with ourselves, as this needs to be our number one relationship in life, because it sets the benchmark for how we allow all of our other human connections to be treated. Love yourself so that when people tell you they love you, you believe it and feel it, not question or doubt it. Like all relationships, you need to spend time with the person, so start to date yourself so that you know who you are, your likes and dislikes, your hopes and dreams, your life lessons, and all other key elements to what makes a relationship tick. For many of you, doing things on your own will be very new as you may only identify yourself as being "the other half" to someone, but you were whole before you met them, and you can learn ways to feel whole again.

Try undertaking one of these suggestions each week, just like the self-care tools:

- Always do your best
- Ask for help and accept help
- Ask "Who am I?" and brainstorm all the words and images that come
- Ask yourself "Does this help me create the life I want?"
- Book a trip
- Breathe with great awareness
- Buy yourself flowers
- Change your hairstyle
- Claim a duvet day
- Cook your favourite meal
- Declutter your wardrobe

- Do not take everything personally
- Embrace your beautiful flaws as there is no such thing as perfection
- Enrol on a course
- Get a pampering treatment
- Get grubby with some gardening
- Give yourself a break
- Go to the cinema on your own
- Go with the ebb and flow of your emotions
- Join a support group
- Journal your thoughts every day
- Love the person who died unapologetically
- Love yourself unapologetically
- Love yourself enough to set clear boundaries
- Make a list of your strengths and achievements
- Meditate
- Nourish your body with good food and drink choices
- Realise and remember what is truly important to you
- State positive and loving affirmations daily
- Say no to others and yes to yourself
- Say "Stop, delete" whenever you go to be self-critical
- Sleep when you need to
- Smell good all of the time
- Spend time on the things you love doing
- Start a journey of self-discovery – the process of gaining insight into your authentic self
- Take yourself out on a date
- Tell yourself "I love you" or "I am learning to love you" every day, preferably in the mirror
- Treat yourself as if you are your own best friend
- Treat yourself to something – you are worthy
- Volunteer for a cause
- Walk outside every day
- Work to live, don't live to work

- Write a bucket list
- Write a letter to your younger self
- Write a list from A-Z of what you are grateful for
- Write yourself a love note

Self-Healing Touch

Self-healing touch is about developing the ability to heal yourself energetically through the sense of touch. Our body is capable of healing, as we have witnessed through mouth ulcers, cuts or post-surgery recovery. From skin cells to memory cells, your body is capable of self-healing.

Whilst energy healing may be a new concept to you, tuning into your energy body is a simple process when you work with a focused intention. When we empower ourselves to regularly self-heal and realign, we start to see positive manifestations in our life physically, mentally, emotionally and spiritually.

The sensations and outcomes of self-healing energy are as unique as you, so be open to changes which may be deeper relaxation, tingling, a sense of colour, a change in energy, temperature, mood or mindset.

There are self-healing meditations and videos available online or try the following instructions:

- Position yourself in a comfortable position, either seated or lying down.
- Bring your awareness to your natural breath pattern, paying attention to the flow in and out.
- Keep your breath natural and simply be aware of your breathing in the moment for a few minutes until you feel relaxed enough to continue.
- Quickly rub the palms of your hands together for around thirty seconds.
- Be aware of the warmth from the friction of rubbing your palms together.

- Allow a gentle smile as you are aware of this warmth and glow within you.
- Hold your hands around fifteen centimetres away from each other, palms facing, and feel the warmth and energy between them.
- This energy is always present but we are not always aware, so allow another smile as you become aware of this healing energy created by you.
- Either using your hands or visualising, start to see this healing energy moving up your arms and throughout your body.
- Be aware of any areas that feel different and need a longer or deeper healing. You can dissolve the stagnant or old energy and see it being sent out of the body to be transmuted.
- Continue to move your healing energy throughout the body, returning to any parts that you intuitively felt drawn to.
- Rub your hands together again to reconnect with the healing hands energy if needed.
- When you feel you have completed the healing cycle that is needed at this time, thank yourself and your body for this time of awareness and healing.

When this healing session feels completed, remain seated or lying for a few more minutes, allow any thoughts or sensations to come. Ensure you drink plenty of water afterwards to help cleanse the body further.

Shiatsu

Shiatsu means "finger pressure" and is a form of bodywork derived from a Japanese massage modality called anma. Shiatsu consists of kneading, pressing, soothing, tapping, and stretching techniques, which can all be performed through lightweight and comfortable clothing.

Whilst grief is predominantly associated with the element of metal, Shiatsu practitioners work with five elements (earth, metal, water, wood and fire) as they say we go through all the elements in the phases of transformation after the death of a loved one.

Earth focuses on the self and our most basic needs as a means to get through, such as having support around and in the home. Metal relates to when the family and friends go back to their own lives, leaving us alone with our grief, and emotions like sadness, melancholy, and weeping. Water is fear for the self as well as others especially around mortality. Wood is about anger outbursts often through believing loved ones were taken, or they left you. Fire is vast as it ranges from panic attacks and nightmares through to self-care and family reconnecting, celebration of the departed, and even feelings of joy gradually returning.

Together with the shiatsu practitioner you can discuss which elements are most prominent, and undertake the massage techniques that are most needed at the time of your session.

Smile

Research by George Bonanno shows us that the more widows smile and laugh during the early months of their partner's death, the better their mental health is over the first two years of grief. Now, I am not asking you to don a false smile every time you leave the house, as I am a fervent advocate for authentic grief. I am only mentioning smiling as a tool for health benefits for you, which you can undertake behind closed doors, even if a false smile if that is all you can muster. The weird and wonderful thing about smiling and laughing is that the brain cannot differentiate between what is real or false; it only interprets the positioning of your facial muscles and will release your feel-good chemicals (dopamine, endorphins and serotonin) regardless.

Your smile, whether natural or forced, will not only help improve your mood, but can also lower blood pressure, strengthen the immune system, relieve stress and reduce physical aches and pains.

If you need a little help with that smile, think about what makes you smile; looking at old photographs, listening to a certain song, watching a light-hearted movie, being with a certain friend, or retelling a nostalgic story. Try to create a daily moment where you smile, albeit falsely, until the frequency and intensity occurs naturally.

Storytelling

For as long as humans have walked this earthly plane, it has been our nature to tell stories and inform others of our life events. Storytelling in grief can be divided into two camps: The Grief Story, which includes the death, and the emotional pain of the loss; and The Life Story, which is about the past, its memories and the relationship.

Sharing our story can help us change the way our grief is expressed and can lead us to new perspectives in which we interpret and understand it. This can often occur through the following ways:

Continuing the love and the relationship

The simplest form of storytelling is when we share our nostalgic stories and precious moments of our deceased, as a way of keeping the love and memory alive. It is through this narrative, that we learn to live with the loss whilst maintaining the unique bond we shared.

This storytelling can be spoken, written, painted, or sung, as we create many ways in which to preserve their existence.

Having our pain witnessed

When we speak about our loss we are speaking our truth,

recognising the reality of the situation. As with conventional talking therapies, when our words are witnessed in a safe and supportive space, we feel heard in our pain, and this is reflected back to us in the witness' paraphrasing, paralinguistics, and words of recognition. We are not dismissed or diminished, we are heard and know our story matters.

Revisiting past events

In stories of loss, particularly sudden death, we tend to revisit the past and keep retelling the story in hope of discovering new insight or closure. Our story is laced with questions and quandary as we search for a loophole, change of characters or timing, as if this storytelling will one day lead to an entirely different outcome, whether it is one of acceptance or an ongoing story full of "if onlys".

In my first book, *Positive Changes: A Self-Kick Book*, I wrote about From a Mess to a Message, how sharing your messy journey can help others in their current reality. We rarely give ourselves credit for how far we have come, but one day you will reflect back and realise you have gone from survivor to thriver, and your words can become a survival guide for others.

Subconscious Self-Alignment

Aligning your subconscious mind with your conscious mind is vital for a progressive life. Your subconscious is the part of yourself of which you are not fully aware, whereas the conscious mind is home to our ego and logical decision making. If we are aiming for a specific goal or outcome in life, there may be an internal battle if the subconscious and conscious mind are not in alignment. No matter how determined your logical head is to move forwards, your subconscious will be like a nagging devil on your shoulder, interrupting your positive momentum with deep-rooted thoughts, feelings, and beliefs. It may not be enough to simply change our actions; we need to change that past programming, and we can do this by embracing the positive.

Positive Environment

Your subconscious constantly absorbs information from your environment, so surround yourself with all things positive. Imagine you are a good apple surrounded by rotten ones – eventually you will be rotted to your core by those around you. Avoid listening to the news in the big wide world, and instead focus on everything being well in your inner world. Do not absorb the words and actions of those with lower energy than yourself, instead seek out positivity through feel-good movies, inspiring talks, meeting like-minded people, and reading books that help you grow.

Positive Visualisations

The subconscious mind loves all things visual which is why vision boards (a collage of images, pictures, and affirmations) are believed to be so effective in creating your future dreams. A vision board (or individual images) work well to trick your subconscious into believing what it is seeing is true. Make a list of what it is you wish to create: a fulfilling career, beautiful home, greater self-confidence, worldly travels, or financial abundance. Then, source relevant images and create a vision board or place your visual prompts where you will regularly view them: mobile screen saver, background on laptop, in your journal, on a sacred altar, or framed by your bedside. If you constantly look at the positive, you will supersede the negative collection of images in your subconscious.

Positive Affirmations

As we learned earlier, affirmations are short and powerful sentences that are regularly repeated to positively affect our thinking patterns, habits, mindset, and behaviour. Be aware of what words or beliefs you wish to reprogramme, and create your own affirmations, such as: "I deserve to be successful," "I focus on the good things in my life," or "I have the power to control my thoughts."

Remember to speak the words positively in the present tense, ensure your beliefs and feelings match (it is no good saying "I am wealthy" if you are thinking about how poor you are as like attracts like).

Positive Brainwaves

We have different brainwaves; depending on the sound frequency we hear, this can be Alpha (relaxation state), Beta (full consciousness and active focusing), Delta (deep sleep), Gamma (for motor functions), and Theta (during light sleep and dreaming). Whether you choose to combine positive imagery with binaural beats or to fall asleep listening to the music, these approaches help gently reprogramme the conscious mind, as well as aiding better sleep. Research which music works best for you and play it during times of relaxation, such as meditation, journaling or bedtime.

Talking Therapies

Talking Therapies do what it says on the tin: therapy through talking. This was always the go-to treatment for grief based on the "better out than in" theory that when we talk we release what is inside of us. Nowadays there are so many different variations of therapy available with a trained therapist and they can be one-to-one, a group setting, family therapy, and delivered via the telephone, face to face or via video call.

Talking therapies are categorised under different terms, most commonly:

cognitive (thought processes), dialectical (exploring opposite positions to see how they might exist together), humanistic (the whole individual – mind, body, spirit and soul), mindfulness-based (awareness of the present and acceptance), person-centred (strengths and self-awareness for personal growth), psychoanalytic (the subconscious mind), psychodynamic (subconscious thoughts and our actions), and solution-focused (exploring future rather than revisiting past).

Talking therapies include: Behavioural Activation, bereavement counselling, Cognitive analytic therapy (CAT), coaching, Cognitive Behaviour Therapy (CBT), Cognitive therapy, Emotionally Focused Therapy, Existential Therapy, Eye Movement Desensitisation and Reprocessing (EMDR), Family Therapy, Gestalt Therapy, Humanistic Therapy, Integrative Counselling (or Integrative Therapy), Interpersonal Therapy (IPT), Jungian Therapy, Mindfulness-based cognitive therapy (MBCT), Neuro-linguistic Programming (NLP), Person Centred Therapy (or Client Centred Therapy), Phenomenological therapy, Play Therapy, Psychoanalysis, Psychodynamic Psychotherapy, Psychosynthesis, Relationship Therapy, Solution-focused brief therapy, Systemic therapies, Transactional analysis, and Transpersonal therapy.

Many of the talking therapies have been covered in this toolbox section, but if there are others that have not, or you wish to learn more about one in particular, do your own research into which therapy may work for you and your current emotions and behaviour. If you do not know where to start, do contact your healthcare practitioner who can help and advise on the most suitable therapy for you at this time.

Thalassotherapy

Thalasso derives from the Greek word for sea, and so thalassotherapy offers a variety of treatments using seawater, seaweed, and marine and ocean derivatives such as algae, mud and sand, all of which are cleaned and purified prior to use. Thalassotherapy encompasses hydrotherapy (mineral-rich showers or pools), massages, algae or mud baths and wraps, facials, manicures and pedicures. Thalassotherapy and its many forms can be used in grief for boosting immunity, easing physical aches and pains, improving sleep quality and for relaxation.

The Emotion Code

The Emotion Code is an energy healing modality aiming to release our trapped emotions, from our past, present and future generations. The Emotion Code accesses your subconscious mind through muscle testing (Kinesiology), and having identified the residual emotions and negative energies, they are then cleared one at a time.

Sixty different emotions are divided into two columns (A and B) and six rows (each of which relates to a different organ). You can undertake your own Emotion Code healing through accessing resources online, from the muscle-testing techniques to the list of the sixty emotions with which to work through. However, it may be easier to work with an Emotion Code practitioner, who will be able to undertake the muscle testing without bias, potentially unveiling insight into your life, and your ancestors, that may have been passed down through DNA.

The Emotion Code speaks of a Heart Wall, which is our tendency to putting a figurative wall up when we experience physical experiences such as heartache or heartbreak. The heart is believed to create up to one thousand times more electromagnetic energy than our brain, so when our heart is surrounded by past negative energy, the Heart Wall will be sending negative messages, that in turn may continually lower our emotions, energy, immunity and functioning. Due to the emotions that grief brings to our heart and lives, you may benefit from this form of energy healing, or if you are aware of issues from your ancestors.

Thermo-Auricular Therapy

Thermo-Auricular Therapy is an ancient practice also known

as ear candling, coning or Hopi ear candling, which uses ear candles (hollow cones made of fabric covered in paraffin wax, beeswax, or soy wax) to remove earwax, reducing ear pressure, and help with conditions such as sinusitis, tinnitus, snoring, glue ear, and stress. The Hopi Native Americans (hence Hopi ear candling) used to practise candling for aura and spiritual cleansing, and to cleanse and harmonise the different energy bodies.

As you lay on your side on a massage couch, the candle will be gently placed into the external ear canal where it is then lit. As the candle burns down you may hear subtle crackling, sizzling sounds or popping sounds and other sensations. When the candle has reached an appropriate level, it will be removed, and the process repeated with a new candle on the other side. The therapy ends with a facial massage to enhance the benefits of the candling as well as deepening your relaxation.

Theta Healing

The term Theta in Theta Healing refers to the theta brainwave, which occurs as we awake or are drifting off to sleep. It is within this theta brainwave that we experience vivid imagery, deep relaxation, intuition, and connecting to our subconscious mind.

Theta Healing is a meditative practice that is believed to help with physical, emotional and spiritual healing while both the client and Theta healer are in a theta brainwave state. This shared experience appeals to many, who may otherwise feel self-conscious in being the client with a therapist observing, as both are undergoing the same experience, and with eyes closed, which can help with feeling more confident, relaxed and engaging in the process.

Theta Healing practitioners claim that, through this meditative process, we can change our beliefs on what we have learned and accepted in this life and others, and that we can release the grief which we hold in our soul.

Timeline Therapy

Whilst grief has no timeline, your life has a timeline of events, and it can be therapeutic and insightful to document them. Draw a line from the left to right of a page, and on the far left, write your date of birth, and write today's date on the far right. Start to document all your positive memories and milestones above the line (birthdays, anniversaries, achievements), and all your losses and challenges underneath the line, in a rough chronological order, with the year or your age at the time of the event. It does not need to be in a perfect order, as it is more about the recall and process than anything else.

The benefits of a bird's eye view of your life is that you can see the positive and negative shifts throughout your life, knowing you have a 100% success rate through life to date. You will see how your negative events lead to times of achievements, life lessons, and personal growth. Seeing these life events can increase your sense of purpose and meaning, and help you to understand and appreciate how your experiences prepare you for future challenges. This positive recognition aids neuroplasticity, the active rewiring of your brain where it creates positive changes. Your life story tells you who you have been, who you currently are, and empowers you to take steps to becoming who you want to be in the next chapter of your life.

If you want to delve deeper into timelines, NLP practitioners use Time Line Therapy, which is a trademarked process evolved from hypnosis and NLP. This therapy is based on the theory that we store our memories in a linear manner, and by recalling events, we can transform limiting emotions into positive actions.

Time Management Techniques

Time management techniques are about coordinating tasks to maximise the effectiveness of your efforts, enabling you to be more productive. Whether you never seem to have enough time or if life just seems too overwhelming or out of control, time management techniques can be beneficial in the work or home daily routine.

Be intentional

Make a to-do list, as whilst it may not seem the most dynamic of tools, it takes thoughts from your head into a visual prompt that alleviates stress. As you work your way through the to-do list, reward yourself for the achievement, whether it is stopping for a drink, a pat on the back, or five minutes of doing an activity you love.

Be prioritised

Rank your tasks as urgent, important or other keywords when formulating your to-do list. This helps us to start with the most pressing matter at hand which can bring about the greatest sense of achievement, which can help motivate you through the rest of your list.

Be focused

When you are focusing on one of your tasks, try not to be distracted by your thoughts or others breaking your momentum.

Be structured

Set an optimal time for your task, which may be ten minutes for some jobs or an hour for another, ensuring you are balancing work and rest for optimal output and achievement. You may find it helpful to use a timer to remind you of the timeframes you have set yourself as it is so easy to lose track of time.

Be realistic

When we have grief brain we exist in a foggier state than ever before, so as much as you may be wishing to carry on as "normal" for the sake of your sanity or to show others you are fine, you are undergoing an extensive and intensive psychological journey, so whatever you can do is enough. You are enough.

Traditional Chinese Medicine

Chinese medicine takes a holistic view of the body, viewing everything as a continual cycle of nature, where we should live in harmony with the world as a way of maintaining our own inner health. *Huang Di Nei Jing (The Yellow Emperor's Classic of Internal Medicine)* is a Chinese classical medical text that tells how key emotions cause disharmony in our organs. *Huang Di Nei Jing* identifies sadness and grief (lungs), joy and anxiety (heart), fear and fright (kidneys), anger (liver), and worry and pensiveness (spleen).

We are often taught to embrace our positive emotions and tone down the negative emotions such as anger, sadness, and grief. However, Traditional Chinese Medicine (TCM) believes that suppressing the heavier emotions can damage our corresponding organ and worsen our emotional experiences at a later date, often presenting as rage or depression.

Grief is one of the most complex and difficult emotions to process, but if authentically addressing all the emotions, and in a timely manner, we can learn powerful lessons of personal growth without overly affecting our bodies.

TCM associates every emotion with an organ, a related organ (Yin-Yang partner), a season, flavour, colour, and sound. In the case of grief and sadness, this relates to the lungs, large intestine, Autumn, pungent, and white.

Grief weakens the life force in our lungs inhibiting our natural ability to disperse Qi, which prevents us from letting go, or expanding our energy into the external world. It is common to see people experiencing lung issues in grief, such as a cough, asthma, pneumonia, breathlessness, fatigue, allergies, dry skin, tearfulness, excessive sweating, hot flushes, and night sweats due to low life force. This inhibited lung Qi affects the ability to descend down into our kidneys too, which may leave us feeling vulnerable or isolated, or lacking in motivation and willpower.

As the flavour linked with the lungs is pungent, beneficial foods you can add to your dietary intake include: almonds, apricots, asparagus, bananas, black pepper, broccoli, cabbage, cardamom, celery, chilli, cinnamon, cucumber, eggs, garlic, ginger, leeks, miso, mustard, onions, pears, radishes, rice, sweet potato, and walnuts.

As we have already covered, TCM treatments for grief include acupressure, acupuncture, and massage as they are believed to move on the stagnant emotions in our body.

Violet Flame

Angels, archangels, and Ascended Masters can all be called upon for support, and one of the Ascended Masters is Saint Germain, also known as Lord of the Seventh Ray. The Violet Flame of Saint Germain is considered to be a miraculous energy of high frequency violet light, which is often represented as a violet aura or flame. The Violet Flame is helpful for transmuting heavy energies into higher and lighter vibrations, so it is particularly beneficial in grief and its plethora of emotions.

To invoke the Violet Flame you can simply ask for the flame and Ascended Masters to help guide and support you at this time. Many declare that you have to voice a specific decree to invoke the violet power, but I am a great believer in setting a strong intention, so encourage you to go with what choice of words resonates with you and your specific needs.

As a guideline, you could work along with the following words:

> I call in Saint Germain and those of the seventh ray. I ask you to lovingly surround me with the Violet Flame. I ask that you help [insert how you need them to guide and support you specifically]. I ask that this is done for the Highest Good of all those concerned, and send love, light and gratitude for

these transmutations. Thank you. And so it is.

Repeat these words or your own three times and then trust and surrender that it is done. As the Violet Flame is so cleansing of negative emotions and energies, it is beneficial to undertake a daily practice of these words or your own.

Virtual Reality

We have seen how grief has profoundly changed in the past twenty years, along with the tools to facilitate our grief processes. Virtual Reality (VR) is one of the latest innovations which use technology to create computer-generated simulations of reality, giving the illusion that the VR users are in a projected environment. Through the use of a VR headset, trackers, and haptic feedback gloves, you are enabled to touch and talk to images of your deceased loved one.

VR has previously been used in clinical psychology, and has proven to be an effective tool in the treatment of phobias (including thanatophobia, the fear of death) and post-traumatic stress disorder (PTSD), before being used in the treatment of complicated grief. The use of VR in grief for emotionally processing tends to divide people, with some thinking it is helpful and others thinking it is hurtful. One thing is for certain, the ways in which we grieve are evolving.

Yoga

Yoga is a great way for helping us to loosen and release both our emotional and physical tension in our body, whether it is Emotional Yoga, Hatha, Kundalini, or Grief Yoga, which are all noteworthy in grief work. Yoga does not require any previous yoga experience as they are simple movements that can be undertaken at home due to the vast amount of learning resources available. However, if you felt able to venture out to try a yoga class or one-to-one session, a yoga teacher can guide and support you through each movement for your optimal benefit.

Zzzzzzz for Sleep

When we experience grief, it's common to experience new-found sleepless nights, long-lost insomnia returning, or exhaustion despite sufficient sleep. Sleep is essential for our physical and emotional health, and as sleep deprivation can worsen our grief responses, it is imperative that we seek out solutions. The term sleep hygiene is used to describe a variety of practices and habits that are considered essential to ensuring a good night of sleep quality.

I have suffered with insomnia at certain times throughout my life, and I know it can be infuriating when people say, "Have you tried..." Trust me, I have tried everything but my emotional times still lead to me falling asleep quickly, and waking up equally as quick at stupid o'clock. So, my apologies in advance for the following suggestions if you have already tried everything I am about to bestow upon you.

- Ask if friends and family can stay with you in the house at night time if being alone at night is new for you.
- Avoid self-medicating with alcohol, drugs or sleeping medications that are not prescribed.
- Be active during the day so that your body tires as the day progresses and needs to rest at night time.
- Block out noise through the use of earplugs, listening to white noise, or listening to relaxing music or a guided meditation through headphones.
- Block out light with blackout blinds, heavy curtains, or an eye mask.
- Choose the best bed and mattress quality and comfort you can afford so you are as well supported as possible.
- Create a pre-bedtime routine so that your body and mind

start to recognise the triggers indicating that you are winding down and getting ready for sleep.

- Do your best to eat natural foods and avoid sugary or fatty foods, alcohol and caffeine. Try a bedtime herbal tea, warm milk, or a malted hot drink. Bananas, bread, fish, leafy greens, nuts, oats, pasta, potatoes, rice, tomatoes, and yoghurt are good choices later in the day.
- Ensure you have the best bedding such as your personal choice of pillow firmness, crisp or soft bedding, and even consider buying a weighted blanket that can provide a sense of calm by applying a pressure to your body. These can be particularly comforting if you are now on your own in your bed.
- Have a digital detox by staying away from screens for an hour before your bedtime; this includes a television, tablet, or mobile screen.
- If you are missing your loved one who used to share your bed, try sleeping on their side of the bed, or having a blanket or pillow to hug in the void.
- Keep your bedroom as a bedroom so that it is purely for sleep.
- Pamper yourself, either through receiving a relaxing treatment during the day, or having a nice soak in the bath before starting your bedtime routine.
- Practise meditation or visualisation before bedtime as you prepare to go to sleep. Progressive relaxation or yoga nidra guided meditations can work really well, as can listening to Theta wave music.
- Rearrange your bedroom so it becomes your own sanctuary, particularly if you previously shared the bedroom, as you will still expect things to be the same.
- You could rearrange the furniture or fully redecorate and add your own personal choices of items.
- Set a schedule of when you are going to go to bed, which

may vary between weekdays to weekends, but ensure you are going to bed around the same time each night, or when you normally sleep if you are a shift worker.

- Set your room temperature to your optimal setting. A cooler climate is thought to be more beneficial to achieving a good night's sleep.
- Try journaling all your thoughts from the day so that they go from your head and on to the pages to help lighten your load.
- Use your sense of smell to relax you with calming scents such as a lavender pillow spray.

If none of the above bring you a restful night, do consider contacting your doctor who may discuss other options with you such as a short-term prescription of sleeping medication at this stage of your grief.

And so we have reached the end of this book but it is just the beginning of your new journey and life story ahead. Move forward with the most courageous of steps, beautiful soul. Remember, you have everything you need within you.

BOOKS

O-BOOKS

SPIRITUALITY

O is a symbol of the world, of oneness and unity; this eye
represents knowledge and insight. We publish titles on general
spirituality and living a spiritual life. We aim to inform and help
you on your own journey in this life.
If you have enjoyed this book, why not tell other readers by
posting a review on your preferred book site?

Recent bestsellers from O-Books are:

Heart of Tantric Sex
Diana Richardson
Revealing Eastern secrets of deep love and intimacy to Western couples.
Paperback: 978-1-90381-637-0 ebook: 978-1-84694-637-0

Crystal Prescriptions
The A-Z guide to over 1,200 symptoms and and their healing crystals
Judy Hall
The first in the popular series of eight books, this handy little guide is packed as tight as a pill-bottle with crystal remedies for ailments.
Paperback: 978-1-90504-740-6 ebook: 978-1-84694-629-5

Take Me To Truth
Undoing the Ego
Nouk Sanchez, Tomas Vieira
The best-selling step-by-step book on shedding the Ego, using the teachings of *A Course In Miracles*.
Paperback: 978-1-84694-050-7 ebook: 978-1-84694-654-7

The 7 Myths about Love...Actually!
The Journey from your HEAD to the HEART of your SOUL
Mike George
Smashes all the myths about LOVE.
Paperback: 978-1-84694-288-4 ebook: 978-1-84694-682-0

The Holy Spirit's Interpretation of the New Testament
A Course in Understanding and Acceptance
Regina Dawn Akers
Following on from the strength of *A Course In Miracles*, NTI
teaches us how to experience the love and oneness of God.
Paperback: 978-1-84694-085-9 ebook: 978-1-78099-083-5

The Message of A Course In Miracles
A translation of the Text in plain language
Elizabeth A. Cronkhite
A translation of *A Course in Miracles* into plain, everyday
language for anyone seeking inner peace. The companion
volume, *Practicing A Course In Miracles*, offers practical lessons
and mentoring.
Paperback: 978-1-84694-319-5 ebook: 978-1-84694-642-4

Rising in Love
My Wild and Crazy Ride to Here and Now, with Amma, the
Hugging Saint
Ram Das Batchelder
Rising in Love conveys an author's extraordinary journey of
spiritual awakening with the Guru, Amma.
Paperback: 978-1-78279-687-9 ebook: 978-1-78279-686-2

Your Simple Path
Find Happiness in every step
Ian Tucker
A guide to helping us reconnect with what is really important in
our lives.
Paperback: 978-1-78279-349-6 ebook: 978-1-78279-348-9

365 Days of Wisdom
Daily Messages To Inspire You Through The Year
Dadi Janki
Daily messages which cool the mind, warm the heart and guide
you along your journey.
Paperback: 978-1-84694-863-3 ebook: 978-1-84694-864-0

Body of Wisdom
Women's Spiritual Power and How it Serves
Hilary Hart
Bringing together the dreams and experiences of women across
the world with today's most visionary spiritual teachers.
Paperback: 978-1-78099-696-7 ebook: 978-1-78099-695-0

Dying to Be Free
From Enforced Secrecy to Near Death to True Transformation
Hannah Robinson
After an unexpected accident and near-death experience, Hannah
Robinson found herself radically transforming her life, while a
remarkable new insight altered her relationship with her father, a
practising Catholic priest.
Paperback: 978-1-78535-254-6 ebook: 978-1-78535-255-3

The Ecology of the Soul
A Manual of Peace, Power and Personal Growth for Real People
in the Real World
Aidan Walker
Balance your own inner Ecology of the Soul to regain your
natural state of peace, power and wellbeing.
Paperback: 978-1-78279-850-7 ebook: 978-1-78279-849-1

Not I, Not other than I
The Life and Teachings of Russel Williams
Steve Taylor, Russel Williams
The miraculous life and inspiring teachings of one of the World's
greatest living Sages.
Paperback: 978-1-78279-729-6 ebook: 978-1-78279-728-9

On the Other Side of Love
A woman's unconventional journey towards wisdom
Muriel Maufroy
When life has lost all meaning, what do you do?
Paperback: 978-1-78535-281-2 ebook: 978-1-78535-282-9

Practicing A Course In Miracles
A translation of the Workbook in plain language, with
mentor's notes
Elizabeth A. Cronkhite
The practical second and third volumes of The Plain-Language
A Course In Miracles.
Paperback: 978-1-84694-403-1 ebook: 978-1-78099-072-9

Quantum Bliss
The Quantum Mechanics of Happiness, Abundance, and Health
George S. Mentz
Quantum Bliss is the breakthrough summary of success and
spirituality secrets that customers have been waiting for.
Paperback: 978-1-78535-203-4 ebook: 978-1-78535-204-1

The Upside Down Mountain
Mags MacKean
A must-read for anyone weary of chasing success and happiness
– one woman's inspirational journey swapping the uphill slog for
the downhill slope.
Paperback: 978-1-78535-171-6 ebook: 978-1-78535-172-3

Your Personal Tuning Fork
The Endocrine System
Deborah Bates
Discover your body's health secret, the endocrine system, and
'twang' your way to sustainable health!
Paperback: 978-1-84694-503-8 ebook: 978-1-78099-697-4

Readers of ebooks can buy or view any of these bestsellers by
clicking on the live link in the title. Most titles are published
in paperback and as an ebook. Paperbacks are available in
traditional bookshops. Both print and ebook formats are
available online.

Find more titles and sign up to our readers' newsletter at
http://www.johnhuntpublishing.com/mind-body-spirit

Follow us on Facebook at https://www.facebook.com/OBooks/
and Twitter at https://twitter.com/obooks